EXCHANGE

of

Identity

KAREENA RAY

PARTRIDGE
A Penguin Random House Company

To order additional copies of this book, contact
Toll Free 800 101 2657 (Singapore)
Toll Free 1 800 81 7340 (Malaysia)
orders.singapore@partridgepublishing.com

www.partridgepublishing.com/singapore

For Rajiv and Vivek,

The joy of my life.

PROLOGUE

15 August 1992

The nurse placed the newborn baby carefully beside the sleeping mother. It had been a difficult labour, and the mother lay back in exhaustion.

The pains had started around midnight, and the baby was born in the wee hours of the morning, heralding the new dawn. The baby snuggled in the crook of the mother's arm, gurgled, and fell asleep.

Nurse Jyoti peeked into the adjacent room where another new mother was having her morning nap. She had delivered the previous day, close to midnight, on the eve of Independence Day. Her baby, not even a day old, slept contentedly, unaware of the entry of another infant, born barely eight hours later, but destined to cause a tectonic shift in her life.

CHAPTER 1

*T*hat evening, the visiting hours had more than the usual number of relatives dropping in to visit the patients, thought Jyoti, the head nurse. After all, it was a public holiday, and the euphoria of Independence Day celebration was in the air. The staff too seemed to be in a jovial mood, though Jyoti sensed they were eager to return home after their shift.

Dr Gita had made her usual evening rounds, chatted with the patients, reassured the relatives, and left a little earlier than the usual 10 pm. She had a function to attend, and she somehow managed to keep up with her social life in spite of the busy hospital schedule. However, she was diligent in her work and never compromised in patient care, mused Jyoti.

Jyoti reminisced how Dr Gita had bought the nursing home from a doctor who was going abroad more than a decade ago. Her husband, an anaesthetist, and she had worked hard, refurbished the clinic, reorganised the staff, and installed the latest medical equipment. Gita had got some monetary help from her parents, and she renamed the premises as Gita Maternity Nursing Home.

The clinic took off in a big way and enjoyed a roaring practice within a couple of years. It catered to middle-class and even affluent families in the town. Patients knew they had a conscientious and capable doctor on whom they could depend at any time of the day or night.

Gita was smart, intelligent, and beautiful. She managed her home, clinic, and social life with ease and seemed to have a perfect life. Then, a couple of years ago, there was a small blip on her seemingly perfect life. Her husband of twenty years was captivated by the charms of a fresh-faced young nurse, nearly half his age.

Gita was at first astounded. It was such a cliché, a doctor falling for a nurse. Reams had been written about it in romantic pulp fiction. It certainly was a common occurrence among the medical fraternity. They used to laugh about it. But Gita, even in her wildest thoughts, never expected it to happen to her. Lightning always strikes the other person. It's always someone else who has been in a plane that has crashed. Not us. Never Us.

Venkat had been a devoted husband all these years. He was a few years senior to her in medical college. Their parents moved in the same social circles. No one knew who broached the topic of an alliance, but everyone agreed it was a perfect match.

They indeed had a fairly successful career and marriage. Initially, Venkat had a steady government job while Gita did her higher studies and had her baby. As the child grew up, Gita had more time to focus on her career. And when the opportunity came to purchase her own clinic at a throwaway price, she grabbed it with both hands. The doctor was in a hurry to join a lucrative job abroad and was happy to hand over the clinic and patients to a dependable team of doctors. Gita took a bank loan and some monetary help from her parents and made an outright purchase.

She worked hard, made the right decisions, employed dedicated staff, and managed to repay the loan in a few years. Venkat then left his government job and helped her in running the clinic. But it was her baby from the start.

The staff looked towards her for decisions, and Venkat deferred to her wishes. Sometimes, it looked as if he was intimidated by his attractive wife. But there were no ego hassles, and he was a source of support during the tough times, giving a helping hand when necessary.

Gita's personal life seemed destined to flow placidly. Then the first ripples began. Their only son, who did not share his parents' passion for medicine, announced that he would like to take his fascination for computers to the next logical step and become an engineer.

His indulgent parents, after initial hesitation and misgivings, agreed to his decision. He applied to all the top universities and was granted admission to a premium engineering college in the city. Soon Vinod left home, with his parents' exhortation to stay away from the temptations of the big, bad city, ringing in his ears.

Vinod's departure left a void in Gita's life. But she threw herself in her work and bore the loss bravely. Venkat seemed to take the departure of his son harder. At least, that's what Gita thought when she saw his pensive moods and noted his absent-minded behaviour.

And then like a bolt from the blue, came the news of his clandestine affair with the new nurse. Gita was aghast. She put it down to midlife crisis one always read about in fashion magazines. She had always dismissed that as psychobabble. As far as she knew, Venkat had never strayed before or been unfaithful. If so, he had been very discreet. But now, he was going around like a love-struck teenager. Gita reasoned with him and was willing to forgive him and give the marriage a fresh chance. But Venkat was adamant. He wanted to start a new life with his lady love. In a few months, he had packed his bags and left town with his beloved. They rented a flat in the city and started looking out for new jobs. Soon, Gita heard that Venkat had landed a job in a corporate hospital. Well, at least her son had one parent close by, thought Gita ruefully.

Of course that meant Vinod had to divide his holidays between his dad, who was just an hour's drive from his college hostel, and his mom, who was an overnight journey away. Mostly, his dad won out, and Gita ploughed herself further in her work. The hospital had lost an able administrator and a well-qualified nurse in one go! So Gita had lots to do and less time to ruminate on how her life had come to this point. One moment, she had a husband and a child, a house filled with laughter and conversation. And now, she was alone in a tastefully decorated house, with no one to share a meal or a laugh.

Thank God for her career, she thought. A place where she could expend her energy and exercise her mental faculties. She threw herself back in the social whirl. Her friends welcomed her back with open arms. They were relieved that they did not have to choose their loyalties between the couple. It is often a delicate situation when friends have to take sides between couples who had split. Venkat had left town and they all pretended he had gone on a long holiday.

I guess that's what it is, thought Gita. Venkat was taking a break from the pleasant but monotonous marriage. Their married life had settled into a comfortable but predictable routine. And Gita was at peace with her life. But Venkat wanted a change. He probably resented playing second fiddle to her in the clinic. He seemed to enjoy the adulation of the wide-eyed young nurse. It made him feel in charge. That's what he was doing. Taking charge of the relationship, and making a new life for himself.

She couldn't grudge him his happiness. At times, she felt she should just be grateful for the twenty years of support and companionship he had given her. Now it was time to let go if he so wished. A glass can be considered either half-full or half-empty. One should be thankful for what one has had, rather than ponder over what one has lost, she thought philosophically!

So Gita put back the pieces of her life with as much equanimity as possible under the circumstances. She resolved not to let the hurt, pain, and loneliness be shown to the world. She put up a brave front and immersed herself in her work. Only her head nurse, Jyoti, who was there since the inception of the clinic, was aware of the turmoil she was going through.

Although only a couple of years older than Gita, she seemed of an older generation. She had married young and had kids early. Her two daughters had been married off, and she lived with her husband, a retired government clerk. She alternated between a bossy and maternal attitude towards the staff and assumed an air of proprietorship over the nursing home. Even the visiting doctors deferred to her.

Jyoti glanced at the clock. It was nearing midnight. Time to wind up, she decided. Then she heard heavy footsteps in the corridor. A visibly flustered gentleman entered her office. She recognised Mr Khan, the husband of the patient who had delivered the previous day. He had a family emergency, he explained, which entailed him leaving town the next morning. He thus wished to have his wife and newborn baby discharged immediately. Jyoti explained to him that three to five days of hospitalisation post-delivery was the norm. Only in special cases could the mother and baby be discharged after twenty-four hours. Mr Khan explained that his father had suffered a heart attack and he had to fly back to his hometown the next day. While he was away, there would be no one to visit the hospital or do the formalities of his wife's discharge. Her mother would look after her at home but would be unable to make the trips to the hospital in his absence.

Jyoti suggested that he come back early next morning during working hours so that she could complete the formalities for discharge. After much discussion, he agreed to come in the wee hours of the morning, pick up his wife and baby daughter, drop them at her mother's house, and then carry on to the airport to catch his flight. Jyoti promised to have the paper work ready for quick discharge of the patient early next morning.

CHAPTER 2

16 August 1992

Four-year-old Nisha scampered in joy. She was going to the hospital to see her new baby sister. She had been left at a neighbour's house the previous day while her dad was at the hospital. She clutched her dad's hand as they entered the private room, where they found the baby asleep in the crook of her mother's arm. Mom too was asleep. As Father and Daughter gazed at the day-old baby, the mobile phone rang. Anil gestured to Nisha to stay put and went to the corridor to take the call. He did not want to disturb his sleeping wife and baby. It was his parents at the other end of the line. They enquired eagerly about the health of the baby and mother. Reception was not clear, so Anil walked the length of the corridor to the verandah. He was soon involved in an animated discussion with them regarding the baby's facial features and whose looks she had inherited.

Nisha looked in wonderment at the tiny baby, nestled in her mother's arms. As big as my doll, she decided.

Carefully, she lifted the baby and cradled it in her arms. Definitely heavier than her doll, she decided. She walked to the doorway to look for her dad. He was not there, but she noticed a little boy at the entrance of the adjacent room. A passing nurse was aghast on seeing a newborn in the arms of the little girl. She immediately took the baby from Nisha's arms, ignoring her protestations. Seeing that the baby was wet and the mother asleep, she took the baby to the changing station and instructed the ayah to change her. The ayah did so deftly, leaving the baby she was handling in the adjacent cot.

Mr Anil Khanna returned from his phone call to be met by a wailing Nisha. In between sobs, she explained that a nurse had taken away her baby from her arms. She pointed out in the direction of the changing station. As Mr Khanna took a few tentative steps forward, an ayah emerged from the room with the baby. He held out his hands and took the baby back to the room. His wife Seema was awake now. He kissed his wife and placed the baby back in her arms. 'I will drop Nisha to the kindergarten while you nurse the baby,' he told her. He took the still-disconsolate Nisha out of the room. As he walked down the corridor, he passed a tall man holding a two-year-old boy. Another new father, he thought. He nodded his acknowledgement and went out to the car park.

Mr Khan strode into the room and greeted his wife. 'I have completed the formalities at the office, Salma,' he told her. 'We can leave now.' He gave her a helping hand as she rose from the bed. 'Where is the baby?' he enquired. 'The ayah took her for a wash and change,' she informed him. As if on cue, the ayah appeared at the doorway with the baby. She seemed puzzled on seeing Mr Fareed Khan. The nurse accompanying her handed over a file to Mr Khan. She then perfunctorily checked the name tag on the baby's tiny wrist, S Khan, cut it off expertly with the scissor, and handed over the baby to Mr Khan. She was unaware that the curve of the baby's wrist had bent the last two alphabets of the name out of the line of her vision.

'Don't forget to return for the baby's vaccination,' she informed him.

'I will,' he promised. With his baby in one arm and his son clutching his other arm, Fareed made his way out. The ayah helped his wife and accompanied them to the car. She waved them good bye, a smile on her lips but a frown deepening her brow. Ayah Yadamma slowly made her way back to the room. Her night shift was over, and she needed to change and get back to her home.

As she passed the corridor, she peeked into Seema Khanna's room. She was nursing the baby, and all seemed peaceful. Yadamma shrugged off her misgivings, collected her bags, and made a quick exit. She would never know that the evening nurse would snip off the baby's name tag after a cursory glance at it confirmed that it matched the mother's name S Khanna.

CHAPTER 3

15 August 2010

*T*he day dawned bright and early. Asha awoke with a smile. It was her eighteenth birthday. It was something to smile about. While the country was celebrating Independence Day, she could today celebrate her freedom in more ways than one. From now onwards, she was free to make her own decisions, vote and marry as she wished. Not that anyone stopped her or prevented her from doing as she wished, she thought wryly, but it was good to know that she could now officially do as she pleased! The thought pleased her so much that she almost went back to sleep. I am not a morning person, she decided. Her mother had described to her how she had been born at the crack of dawn. She probably hopes I would keep it up and wake daily by sunrise, ruefully thought Asha. But Asha was a night person, at her element when all were asleep. Come midnight and there was not a yawn from her, even as a child, much to the exasperation of her parents. But she could happily sleep till noon if not forced by family members to wake up. However, today all would leave her alone. It was a Sunday and her birthday too.

The shrieking of the phone roused Asha from her pleasant reverie. Her first instinct was to ignore it as none of her friends would ring up at the unearthly hour of just 10 am. Secondly, they would call her on her mobile and not the family landline. Then she remembered her naani could be calling long distance to wish her. Although her naani owned a cell phone, she was wary of using it and still preferred the bulky landline instrument.

Asha rose from her bed, opened her door, and reached out for the phone in the corridor. Her dad had beaten her to it and was already on the line from his bedroom. Anyway, it would save her dad the trouble of buzzing her after his conversation, thought Asha as she picked up the phone. She was surprised to find the female voice at the other end, conversing with her dad, was not that of her naani. She was about to replace the receiver when a phrase caught her attention. The caller was enquiring about the details of her birthplace. Her father confirmed she had been born in the town of Hymbai, about eighteen years ago to the day.

There was a pause at the other end, and another female voice took over. She identified herself as a doctor from Gita Nursing Home.

'Yes, that's where my daughter was born,' exclaimed Mr Khanna.

'I am sorry, I could have some disturbing news,' replied the caller.

'Regarding what?' inquired Mr Khanna politely.

'Well, we are investigating a possibility that an interchange of two baby girls could have occurred in this nursing home some years ago,' replied the calm voice at the other end.

'And what has that got to do with me?' exclaimed Anil sharply.

'Well', continued the same calm voice, 'It happened eighteen years ago, and it could involve your daughter.'

'My daughter?' repeated Anil blankly. How? Not possible, he thought feebly. Then he brightened visibly. 'Hey, this is a crank call, isn't it? It's her birthday, so some fun at my expense? Or is it a new gimmick of a reality TV show?' There was an ominous silence at the other end of the line and then a grave voice.

'We are extremely sorry, Mr Khanna, for disturbing you. But a matter has been brought to our notice, and we wish to resolve it. We are aware it's your child's birthday today, so we won't take up anymore of your time for now.'

'Yes, I cannot deal with any situation now. I will call you tomorrow,' replied a bewildered Anil.

'That is fine Mr Khanna. We will be expecting your call. In fact if you can make it convenient to come down to Hymbai it will help settle matters and expedite the enquiry'.

'I will think about it,' muttered Anil, 'Good bye for now'.

'Goodbye Mr Khanna and once again sorry for taking up your time'.

Mr Khanna slowly replaced the receiver. He glanced at his wife who was ostensibly reading the morning papers. But with the tilt of her head, he knew she had been following the conversation. At least his half of it.

'Well, what is it?' she finally asked in exasperation when it became apparent he did not intend to discuss the teleconversation.

'Nothing much,' he said. 'Could be a hoax call'.

'About what?' she demanded.

'I don't know exactly,' he replied hesitantly. 'We will discuss it later.'

Asha carefully replaced the receiver and tiptoed to her room. She tried to make sense of the conversation. The baby referred to, born eighteen years ago, definitely meant her. Not her sister Nisha, born twenty-two years earlier. She wondered if any of her friends were making a hoax call but dismissed the thought as soon as it cropped up. No one among her circle of her friends would do such a stupid thing. Besides, with the prevalent caller identity feature, the source could be traced and it would cause embarrassment to the perpetrator.

She was still ruminating about the call when her mobile rang. It was her friend Neeta wishing her a happy birthday. The girls giggled and chatted for a while. They had been best friends since first grade and shared all their secrets and crushes with each other. Well almost. There were some things better left unsaid. Like Asha's secret crush on Neeta's brother, Ramesh, older than them by six years. He had always been there, a distant figure during her growing years. But he was nothing more than a classmate's sibling then, someone to be greeted when you entered their house and someone whose presence was not even missed when he left home to join college in another town.

But when he returned home on vacation, it was another matter. Neeta's parents invariably gave a party when Ramesh came down after his yearly exams. It was to celebrate his passing to the next year and sharing with the neighbours his grades and accomplishments.

Asha would gaze from afar at this tall handsome brother of her friend. He had an easy-going manner and a casual air about him. He politely answered queries from his parents' friends, even though the same question was repeated by various aunts and uncles. Asha did not have anything to ask him. She was tongue-tied in his presence. Even her greetings were strained. She would then busy herself in the kitchen, helping Neeta set the table and serve the food, while he was the centre of attention among the guests. He probably thinks I am a nitwit, thought Asha. Her heart would be filled with trepidation if she had to visit Neeta's house during Ramesh's stay. What if he answered the door and she blushed or, worse still, swooned? Would he hear the thudding of her heart as she casually asked for Neeta?

However, most of her apprehensions were unfounded. Usually, Neeta's mom or the servant maid answered the door. Ramesh, his attention riveted on the TV, would barely glance in her direction. Sometimes, he would nod at her or wave a casual Hi. Asha would mumble a reply before rushing to Neeta's room. Sometimes, he was not even at home. Asha did not know whether she was disappointed or relieved! When Ramesh returned to his college after his summer vacation, the trips to Neeta's house were fraught with much less tension!

But before one knew it, Ramesh had completed his engineering course and returned to his parental home. He was in the process of looking out for a job and simultaneously applying to various universities for a master's degree. Now that he was in for a long haul, there was no avoiding him.

The interactions were more frequent, and Ramesh actually seemed to notice her. He asked her about the degree colleges she was applying to and the courses she intended to select. Maybe he is just making polite conversation, thought Asha initially, or gathering information for his sister who was also in the same process of applying to colleges. But as days passed, there was no denying that he seemed to take a keen interest in her. Ramesh was surprised to see the straggly little girl who tagged along with his baby sister had grown up to be a real beauty. She was slim with expressive eyes, which always seemed lowered. She hardly met his gaze, and he was determined to engage her in conversation so she would look at him directly. He did not know that he had such an unnerving effect on her.

It was a few weeks later that they inadvertently met at a mall. Ramesh had gone to buy some music CDs and happened to notice her browsing through some books at the adjacent bookstore. He entered it though he had no intention of purchasing a book. She gave a start on noticing him. She had been intently devouring the pages of the novel *Eat Pray Love*, the latest best-seller to hit the stands. He smiled to put her at ease and mentioned he was looking for a good read and asked her if she could suggest anything. They were joined by a plump girl who had been eyeing them intently from down the aisle. As she walked towards them, Asha introduced her to Ramesh as her elder sister, Nisha. To Nisha's enquiring glance, she mentioned that Ramesh was her friend Neeta's brother. This seemed to satisfy Nisha, who wandered back to the section of books which interested her.

Unlike Asha, she was not a voracious reader. Right now, she was looking at some cookery books. She wanted to try out some continental dishes at home as she was tired of the *ghee*-laden, heavy Punjabi food cooked in her home. Asha and Ramesh chatted amiably about books and their favourite authors. Her diffidence was gone, and she seemed much at ease discussing books. She was surprised to know that he had not yet read the recent best-seller novel by an Indian author which had won the Booker Prize. 'It is a must read for every well-to-do Indian who employs servants at home,' she declared. He agreed to purchase it there and then at the bookstore, but she stopped him saying she had the book at home and she would lend it to him.

'Let me purchase this one for you then,' he said, eyeing he book in her hand.

'No,' she said, 'I buy a book every month from my allowance and have shortlisted this book for now.' They agreed to meet the next weekend at the bookstore to exchange the books. Somehow, neither of them thought of mentioning the rendezvous with their respective siblings. After all, it was just supposed to be an innocuous meeting at the mall to hand over a book. But once there, things took a different turn. Ramesh enquired about the book she had purchased the previous week. She raved about it. Ramesh informed her that the movie based on the book was running in the multiplex theatre of the mall. He suggested they go and see the movie. Impulsively, she agreed. They went to the theatre section of the mall and found the show starting an hour later.

They purchased the tickets, which were luckily available in spite of the fact that it was a weekend and a top-notch actress like Julia Roberts was starring in the title role. Asha then rang up home to inform them that she would be back late. She explained that she had run into some friends at the mall and that they would be watching a movie. Asha did not see the necessity to mention which friend, and neither did her mother question her about it. 'Ok, have fun dear,' her mother had replied.

Ramesh and Asha went into the coffee shop to kill time till the start of the movie. They had an animated discussion regarding the recent movies they had seen and the books they had read. They were so engrossed in the conversation that they did not notice the passing of the time. When realisation struck, they paid the bill in a hurry, told the surprised waiter to keep the change, and rushed back to the theatre. They had missed a quarter of an hour of the movie. Giggling, they entered the theatre and fumbled in the dark to find their seats, much to the annoyance of the other spectators. At the end of the movie, Ramesh declared that the next time, they should come well in advance. Asha looked surprised. She had not thought of a next time. In fact, seeing this movie was an unexpected and impromptu decision. But it seemed the most natural thing in the world to meet again. She nodded her agreement and left the choice of the film to him. She was pleasantly surprised to receive an SMS from him the following week detailing the time of their meeting for the film. There was no need to mention the location. It was always at the same bookstore at the mall. This time, the movie was about dreams. Asha watched the movie in a daze, not knowing when reality ended and the dreams of the protagonist started. She caught herself thinking that maybe this too was a dream. She couldn't believe she was actually watching a movie with Ramesh, someone she had only idolised from afar till now. The movie did not interest her, and it could not hold her attention. But Ramesh seemed fascinated by it. He declared that it was one of the best movies he had seen. This time, they went to the coffee shop *after* the movie. It gave Ramesh the opportunity to explain the intricacies of the movie to her. Asha listened avidly and marvelled at the sharpness of his mind, which had grasped all the nuances of the complicated plot. As they left the mall Ramesh, casually mentioned, 'So same time next week.'

Once again, Asha nodded her agreement without any hesitation. This time, there was no need for a reminder SMS. They had fallen into the habit of meeting at the same place and same time every weekend. Sometimes, they just browsed the music shops and bookstores or did window shopping. Even if they did occasionally bump into an acquaintance, it was no big deal. The friend too assumed that they too had met inadvertently at the mall. The neighbourhood mall was a place where people went solo or in groups for shopping or entertainment. Asha had been frequenting it since it came up about five years ago. It was just a couple of blocks from her house, and she did not have to be dropped or require any form of transport to frequent it. She had often come solo, for her shopping needs or just to browse through the latest best-sellers. There were times she had devoured an entire novel in the bookshop itself! These were the slim novels, mostly celebrity tell all, which did not merit deep reading or a purchase according to Asha. This bookstore had a relaxed policy regarding customers browsing and reading books. In fact, there was a section at the far end where customers could actually sit and read a book without any disturbance. Asha knew of some bookstores which sealed the latest novels so one could not even flip the pages. And the eagle eyes of the proprietor seemed to be on you and expressed dismay if he thought one was taking too much time in selecting a book. But the bookstore at the mall seemed to follow the Western line of thinking where they gave the customers a long rope and ample time to make up their minds. Very few abused the system, and there were probably many more unintended purchases, as booklovers got a taste of new and unknown authors.

Asha's mother was used to the fact that her daughter spent a lot of time at the mall. She did not object to it at all and was aware she was mostly in the bookstore. In the early days, when the mall had just come up in the vicinity of their neighbourhood, they had often gone together as a family. They had to literally drag Asha out from the bookstores, where she would be devouring books, unmindful of the fact that her mom and sis were waiting. Her mom wished to do shopping for clothes. Selecting designer outfits for herself and her daughters consumed a lot of time. And Nisha would be waiting impatiently to sample meals in the food court. They had to drag her out before she devoured all the fast food on the menu, thought Seema wryly. She smiled as she thought of the differing tastes of her daughters. One devoured books and the other meals. But nowadays, Nisha had become self-conscious of her weight and was on to some serious dieting. She visited the mall less often so that she could maintain her resolve of dieting. In fact, she had just bought some dietary cookbooks and was experimenting with cooking low-calorie meals at home. This grounded her at home and gave her less time to go out. On the other hand, Asha seemed to be visiting the mall more often than usual, thought Seema. Although Seema herself did not read books much, except for the occasional magazine, she appreciated and encouraged her younger daughter's love for reading. She found no reason to curtail the time she spent in the mall bookshop.

Asha and Ramesh's casual friendship and weekend meetings carried on unhindered for the following months. Neither of them thought it necessary to tell their siblings about it. They might read more into it than required. And telling their parents was totally out of the question. They would definitely freak out. They would not understand that this was just a casual friendship. And that's what Asha regarded it as. But a couple of weeks back, an inadvertent conversation led to a change in the tone of their relationship. They had been strolling idly in the mall, killing time before the start of the movie. They wandered into a furniture shop which displayed intricately carved pieces. They admired the plush sofa sets and glass-topped dining tables. Ramesh declared that a particular sofa set with just a small band of intricate carving as the framework was to his liking. Neither the heavily ornate ones nor the overstuffed ones were to his taste. She agreed with him, and they continued further to admire the dining table sets. An elegant glass-topped four-seater caught their eye. The base was like a trunk of a tree on which was fitted a heavy-duty glass top. They marvelled at the simplicity of the design and the exquisite carving of the accompanying chairs. 'I think we should have this in our home,' declared Ramesh. Asha looked up in surprise. Which home?

Ramesh's eyes too widened as realisation struck regarding the words he had just uttered. He had not really intended it to come out like that. They had never acknowledged any feeling for each other. They were friends who liked spending time with each other. It never occurred to them that being together for ever was probably the next step and logical conclusion of the relationship.

So that was it. There was no formal proposal. It was assumed that they would be together sometime in the near future. Asha's head was spinning as she followed Ramesh out of the furniture outlet to the theatre. This time, they were both unusually quiet. There wasn't much to say. The innocuous remark of Ramesh had said it all. It's the most unromantic proposal of all, thought Asha. But then she realised she wanted nothing more than to spend the rest of her life with Ramesh.

A day later, she was racked with doubts. What if she was reading too much into his casual statement? Was he having second thoughts about his offhand remark? Would he be rueing his poor choice of words? The week passed slowly for Asha. As a matter of course, they never communicated much during the week. She was busy in college during the daytime, and in the evening, surrounded by family members they could not have a private phone conversation.

In any case, they had planned to keep their growing friendship under wraps. By mutual agreement, they met around noon during the weekend, had a meal, saw a movie, and Asha was back home before dark. She did not need to give any explanations at home if she was back before sunset. Her forays during the daytime did not merit any attention from her parents.

The weekend finally arrived, and Asha went at the usual time to the mall. She wondered if he would be there. There had been no word from him the past week. This by itself was not unusual. Only occasionally did he send SMS mentioning the movies being screened, so she could make a choice. This time, there was no SMS.

Asha browsed through the books, but this time, her heart was not in it. With a sigh, she replaced the book. She contemplated going home. She glanced up, and her heart skipped a beat as she saw him further down the aisle. He had an open book in his hand but was watching her, an inscrutable expression on his face. She had no idea since how long he had been there. But he had probably come before her as she had an eye on the entrance since her arrival. Relief swept over her, and pushing away her conflicting emotions, she went up to him with a smile. After some initial hesitation, he too gave a wide smile.

Ramesh too had been racked with guilt since his impromptu remark last week. He wondered if he had frightened her away. He had not meant it to come out like that. But the more he thought about it, he realised he would love to have her as his life partner.

She was bright and smart with a slim figure and attractive face. Although a voracious reader, she was not a bookworm and took an active interest in the events around her. Ramesh, who was a news junkie, was surprised to find that she was aware of all the breaking news and world headlines. He knew a lot of girls who only watched soapy serials or inane reality shows.

He could actually discuss latest world events with her, and she seemed updated with the current news. She had her own views on most subjects and was not shy of voicing her opinion. He now wondered about her opinion of him. Discussing books and watching movies was one thing, but making a commitment to go further in the relationship was another. He had been assailed by doubts the previous week and almost considered not coming to the mall. He could save himself the disappointment of not meeting her, he thought. Instead, he came early and sat in the far corner. He was soon engrossed in the book and did not see her enter. However, when he looked up, he saw her in the mid-section, idly flipping through a book. Something prevented him from going up to her, and he just watched her profile idly. She replaced the books, and some intuition made her glance behind in his direction. She seemed surprised to see him. He stood rooted to the spot, watching her anxiously. After a moment of hesitation, she came towards him with a wide smile. Slowly, the frown vanished from his face, and he returned her smile. Her face lit up.

He could actually hear the birds chirping outside. Everything seemed OK now with the world. They made their way to their favourite haunt and ordered the usual meal. Their conversation was light, but there was an undercurrent of tension. Of something left unsaid. Neither of them broached the topic that was uppermost in their minds. It was as though they had decided by mutual consent that some things were better left unsaid.

It was while entering the theatre, that Ramesh held her arm, ostensibly to guide her in the darkened theatre. But he had never done that before. Instinctively, she snuggled up to him. After a momentary pause, he put his arm around her. It felt like heaven. That was it. From that time onwards, they were a couple, and they both knew it. They decided to keep the info from their parents for some more time. Ramesh knew his parents would not have any objection. Both families belonged to the same state and were of the same socio-economic group. His dad, Ravinder Malhotra, was a businessman, dealing in sales of high-end cars. His mom, Brinda, stayed at home and sometimes did some voluntary work at the local orphanage. She maintained that raising her kids had kept her hands full and she did not feel the need to work outside. She had put her education to good use by tutoring her kids and sometimes giving tuition to the neighbourhood kids. Both parents were broadminded and easy to talk to. However, Ramesh put off telling his parents as he wanted to clinch a job first. He had sent in many applications, but due to the ongoing recession, suitable replies were not forthcoming.

Asha too did not think that her parents would have any serious objections, only the pique of her finding her own life partner. She was aware that in the smaller towns of her home state, a girl who found her own beau was ridiculed or chastised as being too forward. Sometimes, objections were raised even if the boy was of the same clan and someone whom the parents would have considered a suitable match if they had found him initially through the route of well-wishers, match makers, and other busybodies. Asha's parents were broadminded and had left the small-town mentality behind them when they migrated south to this metropolis. Life had been good to them, and Anil's career had flourished. He was now the Senior marketing manager of a retail company. Asha's mom taught at the local school and managed the demands of the home, children, and job with impeccable ease.

A factor that restrained Asha from confiding in her parents was the matter of her elder sister, Nisha. In the age-old Indian tradition, which was ingrained into her bones, it was acknowledged that the elder sister was settled first. In fact, her parents had been actively looking out for a suitable match for Nisha as soon as she had graduated a few months ago. Nothing had been fixed as yet, and a portion of the blame could be apportioned to her comely figure. To put it plainly, she was plump. What was euphemistically called healthy in some circles was called fat in the marriage market. Since the past few months, Nisha too had taken cognisance of her figure. She spent more time at the gym than at the restaurants or food court at the mall. She had also started cooking low-calorie, fat-free meals at home, taking guidance from the dietary cookbooks she had purchased from the mall. She insisted that her parents also eat her healthy, low-fat meals as they too were on the heavy side.

They humoured her, but her mom reminded her that she had put on her weight after many years. She explained that it was a natural phenomenon for the human body to expand over the years, like a tree trunk whose girth increases every year as seen in the concentric rings of a cross section of the tree trunk. Nisha smiled at her mother's analogy. What else could you expect from a botany school teacher?! However, Nisha did not buy that argument. The fact was that the heavy Punjabi food, which was the norm in their household, was the reason they were all overweight. Except for Asha. She was slim and lithe. She ate the same food and had a healthy appetite but did not seem to pile on the pounds like the rest of the family. She probably has a high metabolic rate, thought Nisha as she admired her sister's slender figure.

Nisha realised that her sister was spending a lot of time at the mall recently. But since she herself was busy at the gym, she did not give it much thought. Both the girls were good friends, and the four-year gap prevented any sibling rivalry. Asha was starting college just as Nisha just passed out and got a job at a nearby call centre. The job was considered a temporary phase till she got hitched. Aunts and uncles had been sounded out on looking out for a suitable match for Nisha.

In this scenario, Asha, far younger in years, did not dare to reveal she had already found a life partner. That news could wait till Nisha was fixed up, she thought. Thus, matters stood with neither Ramesh nor Asha in a hurry to publicly disclose their feelings for each other. That could wait till the situation was more amenable, they decided unanimously.

CHAPTER 4

*A*s Asha replaced the phone after her chat with Neeta, there was a knock at the door. It was her sister, who had come to wish her. Nisha had a large shopping bag in her hand, which she handed over to Asha.

'What's this?' asked Asha, genuinely surprised.

'It is your birthday gift,' replied Nisha. 'Open it, and let's see how it looks on you.' The gift turned out to be an exquisitely embroidered designer outfit. There was another box with matching footwear and a clutch purse as an accessory.

'Hey, you didn't have to do this!' exclaimed Asha. Normally they gifted books, T-shirts, or DVDs to each other on birthdays. This was way above the usual budget they spent on birthday gifts.

'I am earning now and whom else would I spend on, other than my little sister,' pointed out Nisha. 'Thanks a million,' squealed Asha as she gave her a hug. She was touched by the generosity of the gift.

'It would have cost half your monthly salary,' she remonstrated with Nisha.

'Well, the eighteenth birthday is a milestone, and I wanted to make it memorable for you,' replied Nisha nonchalantly. She did not voice her thoughts that maybe this was the last time they would spend her birthday together. By next year, she would probably be married off. Nisha was aware of the feverish activity by her relatives looking out for a suitable groom for her. Once she was married, she would come only as a guest to this house. A married daughter was a guest when she came visiting her parental house. An honoured guest, but a guest nevertheless.

Asha's brow puckered on hearing the words 'eighteenth birthday'. She suddenly remembered the strange call in the morning. It had slipped from her mind with the other callers and their greetings. A frown appeared on her face as she tried to recollect the snatches of the conversation and make sense of it.

Sensitive to her sister's mood, Nisha mistook her frown for anxiety and told her, 'Don't worry about the evening party. I have taken care of all the arrangements. I will pick up the cake at 5 pm. The pizzas will be delivered by 6 pm. Your friends will start arriving only after half past six, by which time, I will organise the table.'

'Hey thanks, Sis,' replied Asha.

'You can wear the new outfit,' suggested Nisha. 'It should fit perfectly as I had taken your measurements. Now, come down soon as Mom and Dad too will be waiting to wish you. They probably think you are still asleep.'

As Asha entered the living room, her parents wished her warmly without commenting on the lateness of the hour. They presented her with a small gift-wrapped box.

'Come on, open it,' said Nisha with suppressed excitement. Asha unwrapped the box and undid the clasp. She gasped. Inside was a slender gold chain with an elegant diamond pendant. There were matching earrings too.

'Wow,' she gasped, 'thanks a ton, Mom and Dad.'

'You can wear it with your new outfit,' suggested Nisha.

'Yes, it would match perfectly,' said Asha gleefully. She realised that her sister and parents had planned and coordinated the gifts. She was touched by their efforts. Well, she was the baby of the family, and they always tried to make her feel special. She never took advantage of this or ever behaved like a spoilt little girl. In fact, at times, she seemed so mature, far beyond her years.

In spite of all the happiness and bonhomie generated in the living room, there was a nagging disquiet at the back of her head now. She wondered at the cause of it. Must be the anxiety regarding the evening party. But no, that could not be it. Nisha had said she would look after all the arrangements, and she was always as good as her word. Asha shrugged off her misgivings and enjoyed the sumptuous mid-morning brunch. There was the usual Sunday biryani. In deference to her birthday, there was also succulent kababs, butter chicken, and naan, her favourite dishes. This was rounded up by kheer and gulab jamuns. The cake cutting would have to wait for evening when her friends arrived. It was while Asha was tucking into the gulab jamuns, she caught her dad's eye watching her. She then suddenly remembered the morning call. She wondered if she should discuss it with him now. The way her mom was bustling around the table implied that he had not discussed it with her. Asha decided to postpone the queries for now. Her dad had no idea that she had picked up the phone and overheard the conversation. Asha did not want anything to mar the atmosphere on this day. She pushed the thoughts at the back of her mind and was determined to enjoy her coming-of-age party.

The same thought crossed Anil Khanna's mind. He decided against discussing the morning call with either his wife or daughter for now. It could wait till tomorrow. In fact, he planned to make a road trip to the town the next day. He could enquire about the matter personally and sort out any misunderstanding. If all went well, his family need not even know about the strange call. It could have been a genuine mistake or a hoax call for all one knew.

At quarter past six in the evening, Asha descended into the living room. She looked resplendent in the shimmering blue outfit. The diamonds sparkled on her. Nisha let out a gasp on seeing her. She had been putting the finishing touches on the decoration in the room.

'You look splendid, Sis,' she said and gave out a low whistle. Asha grinned. Nisha did have some tomboyish qualities. Being elder was not enough. She wanted to assume the role of a brother too towards Asha, a protective and appreciative one.

'What are you still doing around here,' Asha remonstrated with her. 'Enough of decorations. I think I am too old for balloons now. You too should go and get dressed for the party.'

'Now that you are here to receive the guests, I can go and change,' replied Nisha with a smile. 'Where is Mom and Dad?' enquired Asha.

'They realised we youngsters would have more fun away from their watchful eyes and have gone for a movie.'

'Very understanding of them,' giggled Asha.

'Well, they will be back just after the show at 9 pm.,' warned Nisha. 'Anyway, we have to wind it up by then as tomorrow is a working day.'

The doorbell rang, and Nisha rushed upstairs to get dressed while Asha opened the door to receive her guests. It was a couple of her college classmates, and just as they exchanged greetings, the next batch arrived. The room soon filled up with about twenty of her friends. Neeta too had arrived midway, and Asha got a glimpse of Ramesh as he dropped her and drove off. It would have been awkward to invite him as all the guests were her college batch mates and he was far older than them. Neeta exclaimed over the beautiful dress and told her she looked stunning. All the girls appreciated the outfit and noted the dazzling diamonds. Asha accepted all the compliments gracefully. She was not really comfortable being the cynosure of all eyes. But today, everybody seemed mesmerised by her. The dress highlighted her slender figure, and the diamonds added to the sparkle on her face.

Soon, Nisha came down and joined them. She had organised some games, and all were so engrossed in merriment that they did not notice the passing of the time. Around 9 pm. Nisha announced that it was time to cut the cake and led the group to the dining room. The dining table was laden with delicious food, and at the centre was an enormous chocolate cake. As the guests trooped around the table, Nisha positioned herself at the far end to take photos. She used the new digital camera which she had purchased with her first month's salary. Most of the girls too were clicking away with their mobile-phone cameras. They sang the Happy Birthday song with gusto, adding a few lyrics of their own. Asha then blew out the candles, which caused more merriment. The candles were of the new type, it didn't drip and refused to get extinguished easily. It took the combined lung power of a couple more girls to make sure all the candles were extinguished and did not reignite.

Now, it was time to cut the cake. Asha looked at her sister expectantly. Nisha handed over her camera to a friend and went and stood beside Asha. A round of clapping and high-pitched squeals followed as Asha cut the cake. Nisha lifted a slice and offered a bite to Asha as cameras clicked away furiously. Then Asha held a slice which she offered first to Nisha on her right and then to Neeta standing to her left. Asha caught herself thinking that was a perfect moment and she couldn't be happier. She had her sister and best friend beside her and was surrounded by her classmates. If only she could freeze this moment for eternity. Then Nisha, practical as ever, took over the job of slicing the cake and distributing it. She exhorted the girls to pick up the plates and start serving themselves. They did not need a second invitation and fell on the table with gusto. There were the typical Punjabi dishes of chole bhatura, samosas, and kachori. There was also pizza, spring rolls, and noodles. This was topped by rasagollas and ice cream for dessert.

The decibel level in the room reduced by now as the girls were busy tucking into the food. They chattered away gaily, and just as they were starting dessert, Asha's parents returned. There was a flurry of introductions, and soon the girls were waving their goodbyes.

It was just after 10 p.m., and almost all the guests had left except for Neeta and a couple of other girls. They were chatting away gaily to Asha's parents, when they heard the honking of the car. It was Ramesh who had come to pick up his sister, Neeta.

'Why don't you come in and have some cake?' called out Nisha from the doorway. Ramesh hesitated but on Nisha's urging parked the car and went in. It was the first time he had entered Asha's home. He walked into the tastefully decorated living room where he was warmly greeted by the Khannas. The Punjabi hospitality took over, and they plied him with a plateful of food.

'Hey, I only agreed to have the cake,' he protested.

'Well that was just the bait,' cheekily replied Nisha. Ramesh glanced at Asha, who stood at the other end of the room. She had accepted his birthday greeting with a smile and now sat away from him with her eyes lowered. He was not sure if she approved of his entering her house. He would have to explain to her that it was at Nisha's insistence that he had come in. And yes, he had wanted to have a glimpse of her. She looked ethereal sitting there in the lovely blue outfit. There did seem to be a shadow of worry across her face though.

Asha sat still as she felt Ramesh's gaze on her. She was afraid her face would give her away if she looked up. Her parents and sister were in the room. She did not want them to have any inkling of her feelings for him. Her family was oblivious to the tension around. They were used to Nisha's chatty self and Asha's silence. It was Neeta who noted that

Asha was suddenly subdued. She put it down to the lateness of the hour and the fact that Asha would have been on her toes whole evening. She indicated to Ramesh that she was ready to leave and found him staring at Asha. Well, you too, Bro, she thought amusedly. Asha had captivated all with her charm and beauty that evening. It was her day.

As they were driving home after saying goodbyes to the Khannas, Neeta teased Ramesh about being mesmerised by Asha. Ramesh gripped the wheel and tensed. He wondered if Neeta knew the extent of his relationship with her best friend. Did she guess at it while watching them together now? Or did she already have an inkling before? he wondered. Neeta was only indulging in some light-hearted banter with her brother. She was expecting a flippant reply, and when none was forthcoming, she glanced at him surprised. She was astonished to see a strained expression on his face. And then female intuition took over. Realisation struck. She connected all the dots.

She recollected how a couple of weeks ago she had asked Asha to come to her place to discuss a class project. Asha had begged off, stating a prior commitment. Neeta assumed she was with her relatives and decided to discuss the project with Ramesh, but he too was away from home the entire day.

Of course, neither she nor her parents questioned where he went as this was his timeout phase. He had successfully completed his engineering degree and was entitled to relax and enjoy life before he was bogged down with the responsibilities of a job.

Neeta recollected how she was so pleasantly surprised to learn Ramesh had seen the latest chick flick *Eat Pray*

Love. She had thought he had probably wandered into it unawares, when the ticket for his choice of movie was unavailable. And when her classmates and she requested Asha to join them for the movie, she stated she had already seen it. Neeta had assumed it was with her family members, but now she knew better. Asha's unavailability every Saturday and Ramesh's absence from the house on the same day now made sense. Neeta heaved a sigh. She had had no idea what was going on between the two people closest to her.

Ramesh glanced at her and realised that she now knew of the situation.

'Why didn't you tell me, Bro?' asked Neeta quietly.

'Tell you what?' asked Ramesh, trying to play it cool. He wondered if he could bluff his way out of this. Neeta remained silent as he manoeuvred the car into the parking slot. Ramesh switched off the ignition and faced Neeta. He had decided to confide in her. She had already guessed as much, so there was no point denying it. She had a right to know. After all, it was her friend.

'We do care deeply about each other,' he began quietly.

'Since when?' she whispered.

'We have been dating since the past few months,' admitted Ramesh. 'It started after I returned from college.' But it seemed like a lifetime, he thought wryly. It took Neeta a while to digest this information. It had been less than a year since Ramesh had returned for good from his college. Pretty fast work, she thought. She did not know whether to be elated or disappointed. Examining her feeling, she realised that other than the pique of not being informed earlier, she was quite happy for them. Both were lovely people, and, as she thought further, ideally suited for each other in temperament.

'If you are serious, why don't you tell Mom and Dad?' suggested Neeta.

'No,' replied Ramesh emphatically. 'She wants her elder sister's marriage to be fixed first before she informs her family. And I want a job in hand before I formally request her dad for her hand in marriage.'

'Well, you guys have really thought it over,' said Neeta and added mischievously, 'Anyway, your secret is safe with me . . . For a price of course!'

'Thanks,' replied Ramesh as he tweaked her ear.

After the guests had left, the girls quickly cleared the table and then unwrapped the gift. 'Hey, this is just what I needed,' exclaimed Asha. All her friends had chipped in to get a single item of value, the latest digital camera in the market. 'You are one up on me now,' remarked Nisha. 'This is the latest model, and mine is already three months old!'

'Ok, girls, time for bed now,' remonstrated their mom. 'It is almost midnight, and it's a working day tomorrow. Dad too has to leave early and has a long drive ahead of him.'

'Why, where is he going?' asked Nisha.

'He is driving down to Hymbai for some business,' replied Seema. 'He will be back by dinner time.' Hymbai was about 200 kms away, and in spite of the new highway, it would entail four hours of driving each way. Asha's ears perked up on hearing about Hymbai. She glanced at her dad, but he had a non-committal expression on his face. The girls wished their parents goodnight and went to their rooms.

CHAPTER 5

16 August 2010

*A*sha woke early the day after her birthday party, in spite of the late night. Her mom was surprised to see her in the kitchen, sipping her coffee at 7 am.

'Good morning,' she greeted her. 'Nice to see you up so early.'

'Mom, when is Dad leaving for Hymbai?' enquired Asha.

'In an hour's time from now. Why?'

'I too will go with him,' replied Asha.

'Whatever for?' exclaimed her mother. 'It's a long ride, and besides, you have to attend college today.'

'Well, its ages since I have been there,' replied Asha. She had only been there once, a couple of years ago on a school picnic. The school bus had taken all the high school students on a day trip to a famous tourist spot in Hymbai. There were some caves with intricate carving on the walls and finely sculpted life-like statues of ancient rulers. The tourist spot was popular among the locals and foreigners alike. The government, sensing an opportunity for increased revenue, had constructed an elaborate garden adjacent to the caves. This was a popular picnic spot for the locals and out-of-town visitors. There was no pressing need for Asha to go there now, and she struggled to give an explanation.

'I want to check out some samples from the botanical garden for a college project,' she stated as a brainwave struck her. 'Dad can drop me there and pick me up on his return.' There was a nationally renowned botanical garden in Hymbai, which had samples of all the common and rare plants and flowers indigenous to the country. Asha's subject was biology, and she did have to make some field trips occasionally. Her mom was still indecisive.

'How can you go alone? Wait for the weekend, and either Nisha or I will accompany you.'

'Mom,' remonstrated Asha, 'I am not a kid anymore now. I just turned eighteen, in case you haven't noticed.'

'Oh I did,' replied her mom with equanimity. 'The balloons and decorations strewn around the living room reminded me,' she said pointedly.

'Oops, I will clear it up before I leave,' said Asha contritely.

'Well, suit yourself,' replied her mom as she heard the honk of her car pool. 'I have to leave now for school. Be careful.'

'Bye, Mom,' said Asha, fondly giving her a hug. She watched as her mom got into the car with her colleagues. Her mom had been teaching at the school ever since she could remember. She was liked by her colleagues and respected by her students. She always made a point of being punctual and never missed a day if she could help it, hence the hiring of a private car to ferry her to school rather than the school bus, which, though complimentary for the staff, was, more often than not, quite late. Asha remembered the not-so-distant past when her life too revolved round the school. The rigid timings, the discipline, and the school uniforms made her feel stifled, like she was in a cage. Thank God for college, she thought. One could wear what one wished. And one could arrive late if need be. No questions asked if one overslept and joined directly for the second lecture of the day.

Asha went back to her room and wondered what excuse to give her dad for wanting to accompany him to Hymbai. The one she had given her mom had just popped into her head at that instant. She decided she could not think of a better one even if she spent hours on it. That would have to do for Dad as well and might just as well be consistent with the excuses.

As Anil Khanna descended to the dining room for his breakfast, he was surprised to see a fully dressed Asha waiting for him expectantly.

'Why haven't you left for college?' he asked her, surprised.

'I have some project work,' she replied blithely. 'I need to collect some samples from a botanical garden. Since you are driving down to Hymbai, I thought I would come with you.'

'Hey, that is a long, strenuous drive. Why don't you get the samples from the local gardens here?'

'No. They have a wide variety of species there,' explained Asha.

'You give me a list, and I will pick it up for you,' Anil suggested.

'No. I want to select them myself,' she insisted stubbornly.

Anil sighed. His docile daughter could be adamant when she wished. He normally indulged her, but some instinct made him wary now.

Although she was the reason for the trip, he did not want her around now. He tried to think of some excuse to dissuade her. 'I will be tied up in meetings whole day,' he warned.

'Oh, you can just drop me at the garden,' she said disarmingly. 'I can spend hours there, and you can pick me up on the way back.' She had thought of everything. Anil had to acquiesce.

'What about your mom? Have you told her?' Anil made a last ditch effort to fob her off.

'Yes, I told her in the morning. She agreed after I reminded her that I was a college-going adult now, who can definitely find a way around a garden without getting lost.'

'Ok, come along,' muttered Anil with as much grace as he could muster. 'And don't forget to get your mobile phone. We don't want you getting lost.'

Within an hour, Father and Daughter were gliding down the new smooth highway towards Hymbai. Now that Asha had got her way, she decided to be on her best behaviour. She gazed out of the window and enjoyed the scenery. The weather was good, and the traffic was light. Thank God for that, thought Anil. He would reach well in time for the appointment. He glanced at his daughter sitting quietly beside him. She was watching the traffic go by with a stillness that surprised him. It was the stillness of a bird just before it takes off on a flight, he thought to himself. Nisha would be chattering away throughout the journey if she were present, he mused. There was never a quiet moment when she was around. And there was never a thought that entered her head and did not come out from her lips. Asha always seemed to keep her thoughts to herself. The phrase 'still waters flow deep' resounded in Anil's mind. He wondered what she was thinking of now. Did she have any inkling of the nature of his business in Hymbai? He dismissed the thought as soon as it crossed his mind. How could she when he had not discussed the call even with his wife. But it did seem uncanny the way Asha insisted on accompanying him. Just a coincidence, he shrugged. He would go to the hospital, show them her birth certificate, clear up any misunderstanding, and be back home for dinner.

CHAPTER 6

The nursing home was beginning to buzz with activity. The floors had been scrubbed, the nurses' shift had changed, and the junior doctors would be making their rounds soon. The waiting room for patients was slowly starting to fill up. It appeared to be another usual but hectic day. Well, a bit busier than the usual busy Mondays, thought the head nurse, Latha. The previous day, a Sunday, happened to be Independence Day, and fewer patients than normal had come. They might have been catching up on the events on TV or ferrying their kids to school for the ceremonies. So today there would be more than the usual rush, decided Latha. She had been head nurse since just a couple of years. Her aunt, Jyoti, who had worked here for nearly thirty years, had finally retired. The natural choice to take over had been her niece Latha, who under her tutelage had picked up all the nuances in helping the hospital to run smoothly.

Latha was the only daughter of Nurse Jyoti's younger sister. She was bright and smart and had aspirations of taking up medicine, but academic and financial constraints made her settle for a nursing career. She completed her master's too and went, for a stint, abroad after gaining experience in the local hospital of her home state of Kerala. She had married just before leaving abroad. Her husband worked in the same hospital as a pharmacist. Even abroad, they managed to get a job in the same hospital and had a pretty comfortable life for a decade. Then an unforeseen accident changed the course of her life. On rare occasions, when they both had a holiday, they drove off to the mountains or seashore for a picnic. On a particularly foggy day, as they were returning, a four-wheel drive appeared from nowhere. In the head-on collision, their little car did not stand a chance. Her husband died on the spot, and she was taken to the hospital with bruises and multiple fractures. Her body healed in a month's time, but the scars in her mind were deep. She did not wish to continue to work in the same hospital. It had too many memories. She resigned her job and returned to India. Her parents had passed away, and her aunt, Jyoti, who was now her closest living relative, invited her to stay at her place. Latha recuperated quickly in the small town, under her aunt's protective wing. She made herself useful in the house and helped in looking after her aunt's ailing husband. He died peacefully in his sleep one night. Then her aunt suggested she could help out in the nursing home. When a vacancy came up, Jyoti put in a word for her niece at her workplace. Latha was accepted immediately, in no small part due to her aunt's recommendation. She worked diligently and was an asset to her aunt. Age had begun to show on Nurse Jyoti, who was now nearing sixty, but she persevered for a couple of years more before calling it a day. Latha effortlessly took over the role of head nurse, and things were smooth sailing, except for a matter that had cropped up a week back, regarding an incident that occurred almost eighteen years ago.

Chapter 7

About a month before 15 August 2010

*T*he Khan household, in a suburb of Mumbai, had been in turmoil since a month. It had all started with a motorbike accident involving their son. That by itself was not an earth-shattering event. Young men did have accidents on their motorbikes. It was a rite of passage. Asif had not been speeding, nor was he a reckless driver. He had swerved to avoid hitting a child. The little boy had wrenched his hand away from his mother's grasp and decided to run across the seemingly empty road. In a flash, Asif saw the child in the centre of the road and the mother's shocked face. He instinctively swerved and hit the kerb. Luckily, there was no other traffic. The child was safe, and the mother was overwhelmingly grateful. Asif had a crumpled bike and a broken leg to show for his efforts. The insurance would take care of his bike's repair, but he had to be hospitalised. The grateful mother and other passers-by rushed to his aid. The crowd, which would have lynched him if he had hit the boy, were now full of concern. They helped him into a cab, which drove him into the closest hospital. He was already receiving first aid when his dad arrived.

Not even an hour had passed since the accident, and everything seemed to be under control. The doctor explained to Mr Khan that it was a simple fracture of the bone below the knee. This would entail an operation to fix the bone in place. The minor cuts and bruises on his arm would heal within a week. But the leg would have to be in a cast for three weeks.

'So he would have to be hospitalised for three weeks?' enquired Mr Khan.

'He would have to be here only for a week,' reassured the doctor. 'After that, he could go home with his leg in a cast. He could then move about in crutches for the balance two weeks,' said Dr Gupta.

Fareed nodded his agreement. He was relieved that it was not more serious. He had been at a meeting when he got a call that his son was involved in an accident and was being taken to hospital. He had rushed directly to the hospital and was relieved to find Asif being well taken care of. After the discussion with the doctor, he rang up home and informed his wife. Salma was perturbed on hearing of the accident. She had always been against the purchase of a motorbike for her son. But her son's pleadings overrode her objections. He promised to be a safe driver and not take any risks. On his twentieth birthday, earlier that year, he had got his gleaming new bike. Salma's requests to wait till his twenty-first birthday, when she would present him with a car, fell on deaf years. He insisted he preferred a bike, and Salma gave in. Now within six months, he had an accident as she had predicted.

'Stop it, Ma,' remonstrated Ameena, reading her thoughts. She was to accompany her mom to the hospital where Asif bhaiya would be undergoing the operation. Her dad did not want to leave Asif alone, so they took a taxi. On arrival at the hospital, they were surprised to see Fareed with a band aid on his arm. To his wife's enquiring glance, he explained that the hospital wanted to check his blood for compatibility with Asif. They might need a bottle of blood in the eventuality of any emergency bleeding during the operation. The hospital did have ample stock in the blood bank but had a policy of allowing relatives to donate the blood to their loved ones if they so desired. This diminished the chances of infection and subsequent litigation. It also helped maintain the stock in the blood bank for the patients who really needed it. Sometimes, the relatives were unable or unwilling to donate blood, and sometimes the blood group of a willing spouse or sibling did not match the patient. In such cases, the services of the blood bank were requisitioned. As if on cue, the nurse entered. She informed Fareed that his blood group was A+ and his son's was O+. While the son could donate blood to his father, the father could not to his son, explained the nurse.

'I guess you could only donate your property to him, not your blood,' smiled the nurse. 'On the other hand, if you ever require a blood transfusion, he could donate to you.'

She had a form for Fareed to sign, giving the hospital permission to use blood from the blood bank. But Ameena and Salma insisted on having their blood tested for compatibility in case a transfusion was required. The nurse agreed and took them to the lab. There was a small pinprick on their finger and then they were made to wait outside. Within a short time, the nurse reappeared and stated that Salma's blood type matched that of her son's. Ameena's was incompatible. Soon, Salma was back in the lab, where her blood was collected and stored in a bottle. It was to be used only if some untoward, excessive bleeding occurred during the surgery. By now, Asif had been wheeled into the operation theatre. Dr Gupta, the orthopaedic surgeon, set about his task deftly. The operation went smoothly, and requirement of a blood transfusion did not arise.

It was almost 6 pm. when Asif woke from his sedative-induced sleep. He found himself strapped on a hospital bed with his leg in a cast, fixed to a stand. He was surrounded by his family members, gazing down at him anxiously. He groggily recollected the events since morning. He remembered braking and swerving to avoid hitting a child and then the sickening crash of his bike and the shattering of his shin bone. He did not know which was more painful. He was in a daze as passers-by picked him up and put him in a cab. He had managed to give them his dad's mobile number before he passed out. He had no recollection of being wheeled into the surgery, his father's prompt arrival, and the subsequent surgery. He smiled at his mom weakly. He braced himself to hear her remonstrations. But she just stroked his hair fondly. She had heard the circumstances of the accident and knew he was not to be faulted. She was glad no one else was injured and the little boy was safe. The doctor had reassured her that Asif would be fine and able to walk without crutches within a month.

It was Ameena now who was chatting away gaily to her brother. To his enquiring glance at the band aid on her fingers, she explained how they had their blood tested for compatibility in case it was required during his surgery.

'And you know', she added conspiratorially, 'only Mom's blood matched yours. Both of you are O+ called universal donors. You can give Dad your blood, but he can't give you his.'

'Is that so?' smiled Asif.

'Yes, and on the other hand, I too can receive blood from both Dad and Mom but can't give to either of them. Isn't that so?' she asked the nurse who had come to check up on Asif's pulse and temperature.

'Yes,' replied the nurse pleasantly, 'you are AB, also called universal recipient.' She suddenly stopped and gazed at the brother-sister duo intently.

They were still busy with their conversation and did not notice the puzzled expression on her usually cheerful face. Mr Khan was in deep discussion with Dr Gupta, who reassured him that the boy was fine and that he would be discharged in a week's time. Asif was wheeled into a private room, which had a spare bed. Salma stayed for the night in spite of Asif's exhortation that he was fine and she could go back home. The next morning, Fareed arrived promptly at 9 am. He had brought some sandwiches.

'Ameena prepared them for you before she left for college,' he informed his wife. She smiled. She did have a hard time inducing Ameena to enter the kitchen on a normal day. But when the occasion came, Ameena rose up to it admirably. Like when Salma was unwell a few months ago, Ameena took over the kitchen and did an admirable job. At least no one went hungry. And all enjoyed the dishes she created by meticulously following the recipe books. She rebelled against having to sit for hours in the kitchen to help her mom make time-consuming traditional dishes. She was down-to-earth and practical, like her dad, thought Salma. Not like Asif who had a laid-back personality and a dreamlike quality about him. As if giving voice to her thoughts, she heard the nurse telling Fareed that Asif was a dream patient who did not give them any trouble whatsoever. She then gently enquired about Ameena.

'She is your daughter, isn't it?'

'Yes,' smiled Fareed.

'Is she adopted?' asked the nurse.

'No, why did you ask?' enquired Fareed.

'Just a thought,' she replied. Nowadays, there were so many options available to conceive children—from surrogate mothers to sperm donors. The line had been blurred between birth mother, genetic mother, and adopted one. Salma felt the nurse eyeing her tentatively. There seemed to be an unspoken question in her mind.

CHAPTER 8

$\mathcal{I}$t was a week since the accident. A day earlier, the doctor had assured them that the wounds had healed well and Asif could be discharged the following day as scheduled. The Khan family were all smiles, but Salma felt a disquiet. The previous night, she had a conversation with the nurse who had initially tested their blood. She had insisted on knowing the reason for her cryptic remarks. The Nurse was initially hesitant to elaborate. But on Salma's insistence, she opened up.

'Ma'am, I am not a doctor, so maybe there are exceptions which I do not know about,' she started hesitantly. 'But if your daughter is AB group, she could have received the A antigen from her dad and the B antigen from you. But you are O+ with no antigen.'

'So what does that mean?' asked Salma.

'According to the blood type, she could be your husband's daughter but not yours,' blurted the nurse. If the situation was reversed and the girl's blood group matched the mother's and not fathers, it would give rise to unwanted insinuation and doubts. The nurse would never have opened her mouth in that situation. But this was perplexing, so the young nurse allowed herself to be coaxed into giving the information. And thus, Salma was in confusion the whole night. She pondered over the nurse's words. She had been so much looking forward to Asif's discharge today, but now that was pushed to the back of her mind. Fareed came as usual at 9 am. They had to wait a while, for the doctor to arrive and remove the stitches before the discharge. As Asif was wheeled away for some X-rays, Salma found herself alone in the room with Fareed. She voiced her misgivings. She related what the nurse had conveyed to her. Fareed did not seem to get it.

'Salma, members of a family can have different blood types,' he explained.

'But the nurse said this combination was not possible,' she replied slowly.

'The nurse does not know what she is talking about,' said Fareed exasperatedly. 'She is pretty young and inexperienced.'

'Yes, she is a fresh graduate. She joined just six months ago,' admitted Salma.

'So don't let her half-baked knowledge confuse you.'

'I guess so,' replied Salma. By that time, Asif was wheeled back into the room. He was surprised to see his parents with such serious expressions on their faces.

'Hey, what's up?' he demanded. 'Doctor says all is fine. I can go home and use my crutches to move around now.' They helped him from the bed, placed the crutches under his arm, and watched anxiously as he took a few tentative steps around the room. Fareed noted with approval that his son had regained his colour and youthful, good spirits.

'I will go to the office, pay the balance, and complete the formalities of discharge,' he announced. Salma nodded and busied herself with packing up their clothes and other personal items. The stay at the hospital was comfortable, but it would be nice to get back home, she thought. She had just finished stuffing the last item in the suitcase when Fareed reappeared.

'All fine,' he said. 'Let's go.' He slowly helped Asif adjust his crutches. And then with a protective arm around him, and Salma on his other side, they slowly made their way down the hospital corridor. The ayah trailed behind them with a suitcase. Fareed too was glad he was leaving the hospital environment. Although it was spick and span, one of the swanky new ones that had come up recently, with the hygiene and décor of highest standard, it was still a hospital. He recalled the last time he had been to hospital was . . . ages ago when his daughter was born.

And then he got a deja vu moment. That time too, he had walked down a long corridor, with his wife in one arm and his young son on the other. And the ayah had trailed behind with the baby. He glanced back at the ayah, and another memory flashed in his brain. He had bypassed a young gentleman, a young father with an infant in his arms and a sobbing little girl by his side. He had nodded a greeting to him, smiled, and dismissed him from his mind. He wondered why that memory returned now, and with such clarity. Maybe the similarity with the present scenario had triggered that memory, he mused. That earlier environment had been recreated today, albeit unknowingly, and the mind had done its job, bringing old memories to the fore.

'What's up, Abba?' asked Asif gently. Fareed realised he had stopped in the corridor and found his son and wife gazing at him with a puzzled expression on their face.

'Nothing,' he said as he brought himself back to the present. Slowly, they continued to make their way down the corridor. But now, it seemed as though they were leading him forward.

They took the elevator, which dropped them directly at the parking lot. Fareed helped Asif into the car. He took the suitcase from the ayah, thanked her, and tipped her generously. They drove home to be greeted by a joyous Ameena. She had not only spruced up the house but decorated it with big welcome home posters. It brought a smile to Asif's face.

'It's like I have returned from battle!' he grinned.

'Well, I am hoping you would do the same for me,' replied Ameena.

'Where are you going?' he asked.

'I meant when I return home after having a fight with my husband,' said Ameena mischievously.

'Oh sure. And I can retain the crutches for him in case you decide to break his legs before returning home.'

'Good idea,' she replied. 'Breaking his legs, I mean. At least, he can't follow me back.'

'Why do you want to leave home at all? You can stay back and torment us,' bantered Asif.

'If you want me to break your other leg, let me know. I am always willing to do the honours.'

Long after the family had gone to sleep, strange thoughts buzzed in Fareed's mind. The nurse's statement echoed in his ear. The episode of walking down the corridor was replayed in his mind, intermingling with the images of almost two decades ago. He tried to shrug off his misgivings, but it was well-nigh impossible. It was early morning when he finally fell asleep. And then he got strange dreams. He was walking down the hospital corridor, and he bypassed a tall gentleman. As he turned around to glance at him, he metamorphosed into a nurse who gave him a cryptic smile. She had a baby in her arms, who gazed at him questioningly. He woke up in a sweat.

CHAPTER 9

*I*t was a week since Asif's discharge from the hospital. He had thoroughly enjoyed the attention he was getting at home. The discomfort of the crutches was allayed by the fact that all his needs were catered to by his mom and sis. Just another week, he thought. Then the cast would be removed, and he could resume his normal life. But today, he had to go to the hospital for a routine check-up and some radiographs. His dad had come early from the office to drive him.

As Asif thought about his dad, a frown appeared on his face. Somehow his dad was not the same since he returned from the hospital. He seemed worried about something. He had a distracted look on his face even during meals. Asif remembered the day they were leaving the hospital after the one-week stay. His father had suddenly stopped midway along the corridor. His face went blank, and he was oblivious to those around him. It was as though he had seen a ghost. Only after a gentle nudge from Asif, he seemed to come back to the present. But that faraway look had never left his face since then. Asif wondered what stray thought had occurred to his dad to upset his equilibrium.

The telephone shrilled. It was his dad. He was starting from his office, and this was a cue to Asif to make his way down to the foyer. Asif collected the hospital records and placed them in a bag. He adjusted his crutches and made his way slowly to the elevators. His mom followed with the hospital files. Asif insisted that he could manage alone, but she would not hear of it. The elevator dropped them off to the ground floor, and they slowly made their way to the entrance. The watchman, Hariprasad, sprang to attention. He solicitously hovered around Asif as he waited for his dad to arrive. He had seen the boy grow up from a young lad to an adolescent in this building. He was a gentle soul and always treated the watchman with respect. The family had shifted into the building premises about a decade ago when the boy was about ten years old.

They were the only family from the minority community in the building. He had heard that they would be noisy, argumentative, and quick to take offence if anything went contrary to their religious teaching. In fact, the building residents too had some reservations initially. Most families were from conservative Gujurati background and were strict vegetarians. Some others were highly skilled professionals, working in the IT sector. Their voice won the day. It helped that Mr Fareed was a senior marketing executive in a multinational company. The family blended in with the other residents, and there was never any cause for friction. A year after the family moved in, the catastrophic incident happened on 11 September 2001. Like the rest of the world, the building residents too were glued to the TV. They expressed their anger against the perpetrators of the heinous deed, but at no time did anyone express any hostility towards the Khan family. The Khan family was equally shocked and expressed their outrage over the happening. Over the years, close friendships were forged, and many gatherings organised. The watchman was surprised to note the extent to which the families blended. Each one helped each other and covered for each other when problems arose.

Fareed's car glided into the entrance way of the building. Hariprasad moved forward quickly and held the door open for Asif to get in. This was not part of his duties, but he did favour some residents with special attentions. It had less to do with those who tipped him and more to do with those who greeted him with a smile and treated him like a human being and not part of the furniture in the foyer. He watched as the car drove away.

Salma had not joined them. Fareed had informed her that his sister, Tasneem, would be dropping in later that evening. Salma decided to stay back and catch up with the cooking. They always insisted that Tasneem stay back for dinner whenever she visited. Her husband, Firoz, had a garment shop, worked long hours, and they visited infrequently. They had visited Asif at the hospital, but it would be the first time they were coming home after the accident. The house was a mess, and Salma set about putting things in order. Housework had taken second place since Asif was at home. Salma preferred to spend time with her son the past few days and had neglected household chores. It was pleasant to chat with him during the daytime, fuss over him, and watch TV together. This quality time with Asif would only last till he got back on his feet, and Salma was determined to make the most of it. Now at the thought of her sister-in-law's visit, she mustered up the effort to organise a lavish meal. Tasneem was fond of her younger brother and sometimes critical if she felt he was not being looked after. She was very religious and followed all the rituals. She sometimes remonstrated Salma and Fareed for giving too much freedom to Ameena. Even if she does not observe purdah, she could at least wear a scarf over her head, she suggested to Fareed. He would have none of it and gave his daughter as much freedom as she desired.

Fareed had arrived at the hospital well in time for the appointment. Asif was whisked away to the radiology department by the medical attendants. As Fareed paced the waiting room, he noticed the nurse.

'Could you spare a few minutes of your time?' he asked her hesitantly. 'I wish to discuss something with you.'

'What is it, sir?' she asked.

'I just want some information,' said Fareed, leading her to the verandah so that they were out of earshot of other visitors.

'Regarding what, sir?' she asked politely.

Fareed took a deep breath, and the words tumbled out. 'You did mention to my wife about our daughter's blood type not matching hers.'

'I am sorry', said the nurse quietly, 'I have spoken out of turn. It was confusing to me, but I should not have mentioned it'.

'No, don't worry about it. But I would like to know more. Is there a possibility that there was a mistake in the lab tests?'

'No, that is not the case. I double-checked later,' stated the nurse.

'What are the options to confirm?' asked Fareed.

'Well, you could do a DNA test,' she said hesitantly. 'There are labs in the city which do it for a fee.'

'Would you do me a favour?' he asked. 'I want to keep the matter private. Could you, on my behalf, submit the blood samples to the lab with DNA testing facility?'

He saw her hesitate. 'I will pay in cash for the lab charges and also for your services,' he added.

'It's not that,' she said. 'It is unethical for me to do that. I am not authorised to take blood samples and slides out of the hospital. Only with the doctors' instructions and patients' consent, it can be done.'

'Please,' he pleaded, 'I need you to do this for me. If you wish I could have a word with the doctor.'

'Then you will also tell him it was me who created these doubts in your mind.'

'No. I will not mention that.'

'But he will guess. I will be under the scanner then. I guess my big mouth and frank nature will get me into trouble again.'

'Well, it is you who wish to get permission from the doctor,' pointed out Fareed. 'I could ask my family to undergo a blood test in another lab and submit samples for DNA testing, but that would raise many awkward questions for me.'

'I will see what I can do,' the nurse said finally. 'We usually dispose the blood samples after a patient's discharge. But since Asif is still returning here for check-ups, we have not disposed it as yet.'

'I will be eternally grateful to you,' said Fareed as he handed over an envelope. She seemed uncomfortable accepting it, but Fareed thrust it into her hand and walked off.

He was just in time to receive Asif as he was wheeled back from the radiology department. The doctor accompanying him informed Fareed that the leg was healing well and the cast could be removed as scheduled the following week.

'You can make an appointment with the receptionist,' said Dr Gupta. 'And Asif will walk home as good as new in a week from now.'

'Thank you, Doctor,' said Fareed and made his way to the reception area with Asif.

CHAPTER 10

$\mathcal{T}$he week did not pass quickly enough for Fareed. There were work pressures and tension at home. He found himself at loggerheads with Asif, who seemed to be taking liberties with his leg. In anticipation of the cast removal, he was trying to balance on both legs and even walk without crutches.

'If you stress that foot and it breaks, you will be laid up again for a month,' he warned him.

'Don't worry, Abba,' reassured Asif. 'I know what I am doing. I am just testing it but not taking risks.'

'Well, next time, you will be strapped to the bed during the entire duration of your healing,' Fareed replied shortly.

'It is OK, Abba, relax,' chided Asif, surprised at the vehemence of his dad's reply.

Salma knew her husband was on the edge. He was normally pleasant enough. Rarely did he bring work tensions home. But since Asif's accident, he seemed to be under some tension. She wondered whether the nurse's comments, which she had relayed to him, had anything to do with it. But Fareed had dismissed that offhand as the prattling of an inexperienced nurse. They had not discussed that conversation again. Salma had been busy with Asif's presence at home. She had no time to dwell on the cryptic comments she had heard. She had pushed that conversation at the back of her mind and did not rake it up again. In fact, she had not been back to the hospital since Asif was discharged. Fareed had taken him a week later for the review, while she had stayed at home to prepare for the evening guests. Tomorrow would be the day when the cast would be removed. She hoped with Asif back on his feet, the atmosphere in the household would return to normal.

The only one unaware of the undercurrent of tension at home seemed to be Ameena. She had continued to go to college as usual, visiting Asif at the hospital in the evenings during his admission there. She was her usual bubbly self, and her presence at home considerably lightened the mood. She gave no quarter to Asif's present physical disability and continued with her verbal jabs and sarcastic comments.

Asif always tolerated her taunts good-naturedly. He rarely reacted which added to her annoyance. He was by nature a calm person, and now he waited calmly for the day when the cast from his leg would be removed and he could resume his normal life.

Fareed had a peaceful night after a week of fretting. He went about his morning jobs with a deathly stillness. Today, he would receive the report from the nurse. The report would probably clear the unnecessary confusion of the past few weeks. Or it could create new doubts. Either way, the die was cast, and he had to accept the results and take it with chin-up.

He had taken the day off from the office so that he could make the morning appointment at the hospital. The doctors and the nurses were at their best in the morning. Their deftness and skill, along with their humour, seemed to wear down by evening. Asif was ready well in time and looking forward enthusiastically to his last hospital visit. Salma insisted on coming along, and Fareed did not have the heart to dissuade her. They piled into the car and left well in time for the appointment. They had to wait a while till the doctor was free. Fareed paced the waiting room till he spied the nurse. She nodded to him, and he followed her to a deserted cubicle. She quietly handed him a sealed envelope. He took it calmly and pushed an envelope to her.

'No, the previous amount covered the lab costs,' she replied.

'Please, I insist. This is for your efforts. Could you be kind enough to interpret this for me?' he enquired. He had split open the manila envelope and was staring blankly at the reports. She hesitated, glanced at his anxious face, and took the papers from his hand. A shadow crossed her face. She blinked. She silently pointed to the result at the bottom of the page.

The DNA structure of Patient C does in no way match with Patient A and B, and they are in no way related.

Fareed's face seemed to be carved out of stone. It was like he had always known the result. His worst fears had just been confirmed. Without a word, he gathered the papers and turned to leave the room. At the doorway, he saw Salma watching him. He strode back to the waiting room. He seemed oblivious to her presence as she followed him. He sat down in the now-deserted waiting room, staring into space.

'They have taken Asif to the surgery for the removal of the cast. So I came looking for you,' she said calmly. He was still staring ahead blankly. She touched his arm. Finally, he turned to look at her. She was surprised to see the depth of pain in his eyes.

'What is it?' she whispered. Silently he handed her the papers. Without reading it, she knew. Her worst fear had come true. She had tried to stifle her doubts the past few weeks. In fact, Fareed had laughed away her misgivings as totally unfounded. So she had stopped pondering over it. But he had followed it up. And the result was there now in black and white. Neither said a word, but thoughts raced through Salma's mind. How could such a thing have happened? She remembered reading in the newspapers about babies being inadvertently exchanged at the hospital. But those would be the general hospitals, teeming with newborns, understaffed and overcrowded with patients. How could anything like that ever happen to her? She had delivered in a private nursing home. They had well-trained staff and fewer patients. They rarely had more than one delivery a day, except for maybe planned Caesareans' on auspicious days.

She vaguely recalled the day of her delivery. Her pains had started mid-morning. Luckily, Fareed was at home, and she was rushed to the nursing home. It was a long-drawn-out delivery, and the baby was born at night around 10 pm. As she was being readied to be taken back to her room at midnight, she was dimly aware of a new patient being wheeled into the labour room. A long night for her, she thought, glad that her ordeal was over. After suckling the infant, she had fallen into a deep sleep. The baby too slept peacefully till dawn. The morning nurse, bleary-eyed, informed her that the patient from the adjacent room had been in labour the whole night and had finally delivered at the crack of dawn. By mid-morning, she heard some commotion as the patient and baby were shifted back to the adjacent room. She had not even enquired about the sex of the baby.

Fareed with tiny Asif and her mom were at the hospital with her the entire day till evening. Later that night, Fareed had come back to the hospital, agitated. He had got a call from Mumbai, where his parents lived. His father had suffered a stroke and was hospitalised. He had to fly back the next morning and wanted the hospital to discharge her and the baby immediately. The nurse had convinced him to wait till the morning when the discharge papers would be ready and signed by the doctor. After some persuasion, Fareed agreed and arrived early the next morning. Within an hour, the formalities of discharge were over. Fareed had dropped her at her mother's house and then left for the airport.

Unfortunately, Fareed did not make it in time for his father, who died in his sleep during the night. He returned three days later, shattered. The baby's presence helped lift his depression. She was a lively baby and truly a bundle of joy. They picked up the rhythm of life, and things were smooth sailing till now.

'Ammi, Ammi' echoed in her ears. The image of the baby faded, and through a daze, she saw Asif walking towards her. He looked so cheerful, and she wondered what he was so pleased about. It looked incongruous in this hospital setting. And then she realised he was without the cast and crutches.

'Congrats, Beta. How is the foot now?' she asked.

'As good as new,' he replied. 'Where is Dad?'

She realised that Fareed was no longer sitting next to her. He had resumed pacing the corridor. Mistaking the frown on her face as worry about his foot, Asif reassured him that the doctor had declared him 100 per cent fit.

'I can resume normal activities from tomorrow,'. Asif informed him.

Fareed nodded absently. If Asif was disappointed at his father's lack of enthusiasm, he did not show it. He was in high spirits as they drove home, and he was oblivious to the tension in the car.

Ameena seemed much more thrilled to see him back in shape. 'So we can resume our weekend treks, Bhaiya?' she asked.

'Yes, definitely,' replied Asif, looking forward to it.

Every weekend, Asif with his friends, Shoib and Rohit, went trekking up a nearby mountain. Earlier, they were a foursome. But the fourth classmate, Karan had left town due to his dad's transfer to Delhi. They had been on the lookout for a fourth companion to join them, but found no one suitable who shared their passion for trekking. Then Ameena insisted on joining them. She was a good walker and did not slow them down. So none of the guys objected. She always remembered to bring along tea and snacks in the car. This was refreshing after the trek down the mountains. They did not have to go for tea to the roadside stall, and they were too sweaty to go to a restaurant. So they tolerated her company and appreciated her refreshments.

They all shared an easy camaraderie, and she was definitely one of the guys. She always wore sensible shoes and clothes, and at no time did she lag behind. She laughed and joked with them without any self-consciousness. She was totally at ease with them as they were with her. Sometimes, Asif wondered if she was sweet on Shoib. She was indignant when Asif once teased her about it. But she did turn red and seemed discomfited by his query. Asif could not decide if it was guilt or righteous anger at mistaking a friendship for something else.

CHAPTER 11

$\mathcal{F}$areed and Salma spent a few sleepless nights after Asif's return home. If Asif was not so thrilled about getting back on his feet and resuming his usual activities, he probably would have sensed something was amiss. He was normally intuitive and sensitive to mood changes of his parents. As of now, he was clueless. He got back to his usual activities with alacrity.

Ameena was of course her usual ebullient and cheerful self. Having her brother home in one piece added to her merriment. She could now continue with her irresponsible ways without a care in the world.

Salma sometimes despaired when she thought of the daughter. She was of almost marriageable age but showed absolutely no inclination for performing household chores. Cooking and cleaning were just not her cup of tea, she had declared more often than once. Salma mused how some of her friends who only bore sons expressed regrets of not having a daughter. Their contention was that a daughter was emotionally close to the mom. A daughter would be a friend and confidante to the mother, in tune with her moods and sympathetic to her needs, they said. Salma saw no evidence of this in her relationship with her tomboyish daughter. In fact, Asif was more tuned to her moods and sympathetic to her feelings. He listened patiently to her problems and reassured her that things would turn out fine.

Things were definitely not fine, according to Fareed. The disturbing news weighed on his mind till he could bear it no longer. Finally, he made up his mind and made a call to the hospital. The phone number of the hospital had been relatively easy to obtain with the explosion of information technology since the past decade. What was difficult was getting through to the doctors concerned. The duty nurse had tried to fob him off and probably did not understand the gravity of the situation. Finally, after repeated calls, he was shunted to the head nurse who put him directly in touch with a doctor. She was more receptive to his pleas to check the records. Within a couple of days, he received information from the hospital that a baby girl had been delivered by Mrs Seema Khanna a few hours after the birth of his daughter.

The doctor was clueless how a switch could have taken place, but Fareed sounded desperate and she promised to make enquiries. She was as good as her word and in a short time had the Khanna family's latest phone number and address, which she conveyed to Fareed.

Now Fareed was in a dilemma as to how to go ahead. He could not approach a family with unsubstantiated claims. Finally, he requested the staff at the hospital to arrange a meeting with the family. By now, Dr Gita of the Gita Nursing Home was acquainted with the situation. She too had made enquiries. She had had a talk with the retired head nurse of that period. Nurse Jyoti, though retired, was still around and stayed at a nearby cottage, which she shared with the present head nurse, who was her niece.

Dr Gita and Nurse Jyoti discussed the situation. They had shared a relationship which went beyond that of employer and employee. There was no blame game in the conversation, just a deep desire to get to the bottom of the problem. They both tried to recollect that fateful day and the events preceding it. Yes, it was on the eve of Independence Day, and there were two back-to-back deliveries. All had gone fine, and there were no complications in either of the cases. Dr Gita recollected that she was able to make it to a social function later that evening. She had just come to terms with the disastrous ending of her marriage. Meeting up with her friends and social circle gave a balance to her life. However, she had never compromised on her duties to her patients, who always came first.

Nurse Jyoti too remembered Fareed's plea to have his wife and daughter discharged immediately that night, irrespective of the lateness of the hour. Her calm reasoning and sensible solution had won the day, and he had agreed to return early morning to complete the formalities. She had related all this to Dr Gita the following day and was commended for her deft handling of the situation.

Now both reminisced about the events of the following day. While what Fareed claimed was highly improbable, it was not impossible. There was one in a million chance that such a thing could have happened. Dr Gita noted the similarity of the initials in the mothers' names. That could have led to this unfortunate mishap. She decided to get to the bottom of it and took a personal interest in the matter. This was not due to the fear of litigation but to set matters straight. Fareed had assured her that he was not interested in pressing charges or creating problems for anyone. He just wanted to know the truth of the situation, which was causing him sleepless nights.

Thus, Mr Anil Khanna got a call from the hospital on a bright Sunday morning. And on Monday morning, he was speeding towards the hospital, with the daughter in question, who had obstinately insisted on coming along.

As they reached the outskirts of the town, he reduced the speed of the car and glanced at his daughter. She was gazing serenely out of the window, soaking in the sights and sounds of the town. She seemed oblivious of the tension eating into him.

'I will drop you off at the botanical garden,' he informed her, 'and then I will go to the branch office for some meetings.'

'And then?' she asked, turning to look at him directly. He was disconcerted by her direct gaze.

'Then I will go to the hospital to meet a friend,' he said noncommittally.

'I will meet you there, after I finish my work at the garden,' she said casually.

'No.' That came out more emphatically than he intended. 'Hang on at the garden, and I will pick you up on my way back.'

'But if I finish early, I will come there in an auto,' she insisted.

'You are not travelling in a strange city alone in an auto,' he said sternly.

She finally agreed to stay back in the garden until he picked her up later in the evening.

CHAPTER 12

Fareed was having mixed feelings today. He had heard from the hospital that Mr Khanna was driving down to the hospital for a talk with the hospital administrator. That meeting could throw some light on this situation. He wondered if he had done the right thing by kick-starting the process. The children had been raised from infancy to adulthood by the families. Both were loved by their respective families. Nothing would give them back their childhood. Instead, it would now create complications in their adult life. A part of his mind had said, 'Let sleeping dogs lie.'

But from the other corner of his mind flashed a long forgotten phrase, *Satya Meva Jayate*. Truth Always prevails. This had been his school motto inscribed in the school badge. He had chanted it many times in his boyhood years, without a second thought. It now filled his mind with electrifying clarity. The truth, however unpalatable, would have to come out. Inadvertently, unbeknownst to all, a colossal error had occurred years earlier. But now, when a glimmer of truth had been revealed, it could not be ignored. The matter had to be investigated. Two wrongs do not make a right, reasoned Fareed and had kept up the pressure with the hospital staff till they had located the relevant family.

Now the dilemma for Fareed was whether to let the hospital conduct the initial investigation at its own pace or to become proactive and get involved. The hospital probe would take time. The uncertainty was eating into him. He had no intention of suing the hospital or apportioning blame. He had made that clear to the hospital staff. They appreciated his attitude and were genuinely trying to get to the bottom of the matter.

After bouts of indecision, Fareed decided to make a road trip to Hymbai. Salma's mother still resided there, and it was ages since they had visited her. He sounded Salma on the idea, and she was enthusiastic. She knew it had to do with the hospital investigation, but she kept her counsel and did not question him further. The spanner in the works was that Asif insisted on coming along. He wished to see his naani and also liked the thought of a long drive. He knew he could wheedle his dad into taking over the wheel during the long journey. Ameena begged off the family trip citing college commitments.

The Khan family started early morning and reached at noon. Salma's mom had lunch awaiting them, and then they had a short nap. As Fareed and Salma prepared to leave for the hospital in the evening, Asif insisted on dropping them. He claimed he had a couple of friends to meet, so he wanted the car. His parents acquiesced, and he dropped them at the hospital and drove off gleefully, promising to be back soon.

Fareed and Salma made their way to the office. They were told that the hospital administrator was in a meeting with a gentleman. They nodded and decided to wait it out.

Inside, Mr Khanna was having a hard time with the hospital administrator. He recounted the events leading to the birth of his daughter and those preceding the discharge from the hospital. He was baffled how a switch could ever have been made.

But as of now, it was established that both the babies had been born in the same hospital, a few hours apart. And the Khan baby's blood group did not match that of her parents. Now it had to be seen if the Khanna baby's blood group matched her parents. Anil stated that his blood group was B+ and that of his wife was AB. They had required to take it as part of the formalities of their medical insurance, and it was mentioned in the card. Asha's blood group was A+. Nisha's was AB+.

The hospital administrator agreed that there was no discrepancy in that and Asha could be their child. On the other hand, she could also be the progeny of the Khan family.

Blood grouping was a very broad classification, he explained to Anil. Further tests would be necessary. If the child was AB+, it would have at the least proved it was not the Khan progeny. A No was conclusive, but not a Yes. Until further tests were conducted, nothing could be decided. Till now, it was only circumstantial evidence. He conveyed all this patiently to Mr Khanna.

'So the blood groupings do not disprove that she is my daughter,' asked Mr Khanna, clutching at straws.

'No,' admitted the administrator. 'But it also matches that of the Khan's, so we have to go forward from here.'

'I know it in my bones that she is my flesh and blood,' claimed Anil. 'She resembles me too,' he added. The hospital administrator perked his ears.

'Well, my elder daughter is like my wife, and the younger one is said to have taken after me,' said Anil lamely.

It was true that Nisha was a younger version of her mom, plump, medium height with a bright complexion. Asha was slim and tall and by natural inference was assumed to have taken after her father in the family lore as she had definitely not taken after her mom. The conversation was interrupted by a phone call. The hospital administrator, Dr Sanjay, received it and nodded quietly. The discussion resumed, but he seemed a bit disconcerted. After a few minutes, he quietly informed Mr Khanna that the presumptive parents of the disputed baby were at the hospital premises.

A silence followed. Anil debated his next course of action. He could have just walked out. This was not part of the plan. Things were moving faster than he expected. He had come down to settle matters, not to raise more issues. The blood group did not indicate that Asha was not their daughter. It had vindicated his stand. It was too bad if the Khan's daughter did not match with that of her parents. They would have to look elsewhere for a matching daughter, he thought grimly.

Even as these thoughts coursed through his mind, Anil knew he was being unreasonable.

And then curiosity gnawed at him. Who were these people who had driven down here on a whim, to get to the root of the matter? Why didn't they just continue to love the daughter they had raised?

Anil knew whatever the results of the genetic test, Asha would always be his daughter. He would never stop loving, caring, or worrying about her. In fact, if he had come across some inconclusive blood tests, he would not have investigated further. He would have been too scared of losing her to probe the matter.

Dimly through his reverie, he could hear Dr Sanjay asking him a question. He shook his head to clear his mind and concentrate on the conversation. Dr Sanjay was repeating the question, 'Would you like to meet Mr Khan, who happens to be here now?' Anil's mind screamed No, but his head nodded Yes.

Within a few moments, the door opened, and a tall gentleman entered. He had a swarthy complexion and an ungainly gait.

There is no resemblance, thought Anil, exultantly. After an awkward handshake, they sat down, and Dr Sanjay explained to them how the blood group of the Khanna girl was ambiguous. Fareed listened intently to the doctor's words while Anil sized him up. His initial reaction notwithstanding, he realised Mr Khan had a gentle manner and courteous air. As they walked out, Mr Khan introduced Anil to his wife, who had been waiting outside patiently. Anil noted that she was of medium build, average height, fair, slim, and had a pleasant face. But there was no overt resemblance to Asha. Not the way Seema and Nisha resembled each other. Well, the couple would have to look elsewhere for their genetic daughter. It sure wasn't his baby.

Fareed's mobile rang. It was Asif calling to say he had arrived at the hospital to pick them up. Fareed informed Anil that his son was waiting at the parking lot and would take his leave. Aha, there is a son too, thought Anil. He remembered a small boy clutching his father's hand as they passed each other in the hospital corridor ages ago. In fact, it was this same corridor. But now, both were walking out together, not crossing each other's path. They reached the entrance and nodded their goodbyes. They had verbally agreed with the hospital administrator to submit their blood samples the following week for further tests. A pretence of civility had to be maintained. Anil couldn't care less if he never saw him again. A car slid into the driveway. A young man got down and handed over the keys to Mr Khan, who accepted it with a smile. As an afterthought, he turned to introduce Anil to his son. Anil stood mesmerised. He numbly extended his hand to Asif's proffered handshake. He noted Asif's pale complexion, brown eyes, and long eyelashes. More than that, the gait was familiar. The long angular arms and legs, which nevertheless moved gracefully. Anil watched his profile as Asif slid into the backseat of the car. That too seemed similar. Similar to what? His head reeled as he waved goodbye.

He had been so exuberant a little while ago. The ambiguity of the blood groups and the lack of resemblance to the so-called parents had buoyed his spirits. The further lab tests suggested by the doctors had not worried him. But out of the blue, the situation had changed dramatically. The genetic testing now seemed only a formality that would conclusively establish what had just become clear to him.

He needed a drink. He needed to sit down. He had been rooted to the spot since his handshake with Asif. And then through a blur, he saw an auto draw up at the driveway. A young girl got down, paid the auto, and walked towards him.

Horror of horrors! It was Asha. Would the nightmare never end?

'What are you doing here?' he croaked.

'The botanical garden shut down early today, so I thought I would meet you here,' she replied blithely.

He was too emotionally drained to question her further. He just stood looking at her blankly.

'Are you OK?' she asked concernedly. She looked intently at his face. He looked like he had seen a ghost.

'I'm fine,' he said sharply. 'I just need to sit down a moment.' They sat in silence on a bench at the entrance.

Anil closed his eyes tightly. It was a day of too many upheavals. Asha's unexpected arrival had unnerved him. If she had come a few minutes earlier, she would have encountered the Khan family.

Thank God for small mercies, he thought. But bigger questions would have to be resolved. That would take time.

He opened his eyes and nodded to Asha. 'Let's go,' he smiled.

'What happened, Dad,' she sounded worried.

'I did not have lunch, so I felt a bit weak,' he said reassuringly.

She accepted his explanation without comment, and they walked slowly towards the car. They drove in silence for some time. There wasn't much to say, decided Anil. His head was still reeling with the revelations of the past few hours. It was more than one could take in the span of a day.

And to top it all, Asha's unexpected arrival at the hospital. Come to think of it, she had been pretty insistent on joining him for the trip. His suspicions were now raised. Intuition is a quality generally attributed to females. But now, Anil intuitively realised that she knew more than she was letting on.

He glanced at her. She was staring forward at the windshield. It was getting too dark now to look at the scenery from the windows. She became aware of his gaze and turned to look at him. She saw the unasked question on his face.

Impulsively, she blurted out, 'Dad, I heard the conversation on the phone.'

'What conversation?' he asked, genuinely puzzled.

'Yesterday morning, from the hospital,' she mumbled.

It took some time for that to sink in. He was quiet for so long she wondered if he had heard her.

There was a fast food restaurant ahead. The car slid to a stop.

'Let's have a bite,' he suggested.

They made their way to the counter and ordered sandwiches and soft drinks. They sat down at a table near the window. There weren't many people in at this hour. They could talk without being disturbed. The waiter placed the food on the table and disappeared. Anil munched his sandwich. It had been a long day.

'So what did you overhear?' he asked suddenly, startling Asha.

'I thought it was a call for me,' she said by way of explanation.

'But it wasn't,' he pointed out.

'And as I was about to replace the receiver,' she continued ignoring his comment, 'I heard the caller ask about my birthdate.' She paused but Anil remained silent.

'Anyway, I heard out the rest of the conversation,' she ended lamely.

'And you didn't think it necessary to mention this to me?' he asked.

'Neither did you,' she pointed out.

Point taken, he thought.

'I wanted to clarify the matter before I discussed it with you and your mom,' he explained gently.

'So Mom knows nothing about this?' she asked surprised.

'No,' he admitted.

'So what happened today?' she asked simply. 'You can tell me now.'

He sighed. Yes he had to tell her. She had just turned eighteen yesterday. And it involved her. She had a right to know.

He told her about the meeting with the hospital administrator, Dr Sanjay. How the Khan baby had a blood group inconsistent with that of her parents. This had come to light just recently as a consequence of some blood tests. And how Asha's blood group was consistent with her parents. But it also happened to be consistent with that of the Khan parents.

Asha munched her sandwich thoughtfully and was silent.

At present, there was only circumstantial evidence that their families were involved in the mix-up, mused Anil. The Khan baby could have got exchanged with another kid at a later date, maybe at a vaccination centre or even kindergarten. All toddlers look alike. Maybe if the pre-school kids were dressed up in the same clothes, the parents would not have noticed if the wrong toddler was brought home. He shook his head. He was getting maudlin. He had to maintain his sanity.

Anil noticed that Asha had finished her sandwich.

'Let's go now,' he said kindly. They were silent on the drive back home, each with their own thoughts.

'Should we tell Mom?' was all she asked as they neared their house.

'Yes,' he replied. 'I will handle that. You go to bed. You have had a hard day.'

Seema was awaiting their arrival anxiously. 'Dinner is on the table,' she announced as they entered.

'Oh, we have eaten,' replied Anil.

'That's why you took so long,' she exclaimed. 'Nisha and I too have just finished our dinner.'

Anil went upstairs to have a shower while Seema busied herself in clearing the dinner table.

Asha found Nisha engrossed in a late-night TV movie. She was relieved she did not have to describe the events of the day to her sister. She had a shower and went to bed immediately.

Of course, sleep would not come. A multitude of thoughts were buzzing through her head. When Nisha peeked into her room after the movie and whispered a tentative Hi, she pretended to be asleep. Nisha gently closed the door and went back to her room.

Surprisingly, Asha fell asleep soon after, into a long dreamless sleep. When she woke in the morning, she felt fresh and light-hearted. The events of the previous day seemed like a distant dream. It had happened to her on a couple of occasions earlier.

She had dreamt that the exam results had been declared and she had failed. She went through the emotions of anxiety and embarrassment. She wilted under the pitying glances of her classmates. She had woken up in the morning in a distressed state. She was trying to analyse the cause of her failure. Slowly, it dawned on her that the declaration of the results was still a couple of days away, and it was all a dream, or rather a nightmare. Relief had swept over her. There was a spring in her step for the rest of the day. Of course, when the actual results were out, she had passed with flying colours. The nightmare by then was a dim memory.

At another time, she had lost her handbag. She was looking for it frantically. It held her credit and debit cards, keys, college id, expensive sunglasses, and purse with a substantial amount of cash. She wandered around all the places she had visited since morning, the college cafeteria and the library. She asked myriad people she encountered. She was at her wits' end. She didn't even know how she would get home. She tossed and turned and awoke in a distressed state. It took some time to sink in that she was already at home and that the entire episode was just a dream or rather a nightmare.

Still she made the effort to raise her head and glance at the dressing table where her handbag was comfortably resting, to reassure herself that it was a dream. Oh why hadn't I realised that it was a dream when I was wandering the streets looking for my purse? she thought regretfully. It would have saved her a lot of stress!

Today, as she lay on her bed ruminating, the events of the previous day seeped into her memory. She wondered groggily whether it was a dream or for real. In the half-awakened state, she really had no idea. Earlier too, the nightmares had seemed so real.

Once she had even pinched herself in her dream, acknowledged that the event was really happening, and yet got up in the morning to realise that it was a dream after all. Now she had to really concentrate. She remembered her birthday party and her friends coming home. And then there was a long drive. Her dad was driving. He was at times irritable, then angry, and then comforting. She racked her brains to recollect what it was all about. Slowly, the memories seeped in, the phone call she had eavesdropped on and her insistence on going along with her dad, for, well, just the fun of it. An adventure and a story to relate. It was on this drive back that she sensed something was wrong. Although her dad assured her that her blood group was consistent with her parents, and that it was a long shot that any exchange of babies involving her ever took place, she felt a disquiet in him. It was as though he did not believe in his own words. She wondered what had stunned him when she had arrived unexpectedly at the hospital. It could not have been just her unexpected arrival. He had seemed disoriented even before he had seen her. With a sigh, Asha realised all the events of the previous day had actually happened. She could pinch herself back and blue, but the nightmare would not end. It was not a dream. It was all, oh, so true!

She wondered about her dad's mental state this morning. And she wondered if he had conveyed the situation to her mom.

CHAPTER 13

$\mathcal{T}$he Khannas had had a rough night.

Seema, on entering her room, after clearing the dinner table, late last night, was pleasantly surprised to see Anil, relaxing on his easy chair. Normally, he would be on the computer, reading email or checking the market updates. Or he would have switched on the TV and got engrossed in the news of the day or a movie. If she ever had to discuss any domestic matters, at the end of the day, it was a difficult job to pry him away from the TV or computer and get his full attention. With both of them working at full-time jobs, spending quality time with each other was a rarity. There was hardly any opportunity to hold a conversation during the daytime without interruptions from the children or household help. Since the matters mostly concerned them, Seema could do without their helpful suggestions. She cherished the post-dinner conversation with her husband, but with 24 × 7 cable TV and the explosion of content on the Internet, it was a rarity to find him free. But tonight, he was sitting still and doing nothing.

'Had a hard day, is it?' she smiled questioningly at him. He nodded and looked up. She was surprised to see the weariness on his face.

'Sit down, there is something I have to talk to you about,' he said quietly.

It was a long night. He did not conceal anything from her. He explained about the initial phone call which had perplexed him the previous day and then the meeting with the hospital administrator. He described his joy on learning that Asha's blood group was consistent with theirs to the shock on meeting Asif.

Seema was silent for most of the story and then bewildered. How and when could an exchange of babies have occurred? How was it possible she had not noticed? She tried to recollect the sequence of events at the hospital. After a night consumed with labour pains, she had finally delivered in the wee hours of the morning. She then had a long nap and awakened only in the evening. The first night was stressful as she had to feed the baby intermittently. It was only in the morning the baby and she fell into a fitful sleep. When she opened her eyes, she found Anil cradling the baby and a sobbing Nisha. As she had not seen Nisha since the onset of her labour pains, she reached out to her first and hugged her tight. To her enquiring glance, Anil explained that she had been holding the baby when a nurse had peremptorily taken it away from her. And when the nurse had walked across to the changing station on finding the baby wet, Nisha had felt she was taking away her baby. Seema had smiled and hugged Nisha. The newborn was dry and content and cooed happily in Anil's arms. So Seema gave all her attention to Nisha, who described her day at the neighbour's house the previous evening. Anil paced the corridor with the baby and allowed Seema time with her first born. Then it was time for Nisha to go to school. Anil placed the infant gently in the baby cot, took Nisha firmly by the hand, and they said their goodbyes. Seema rested a while before the interminable rounds of feeding and changing the baby.

As Seema reminisced about the past events, she wondered if there was a mix-up when the nurse took the baby for a diaper change to the changing station. No, she would have realised when the baby was returned. Or would she? The exhaustion and drugs would have dulled her senses. She sighed. That was such a long time ago.

CHAPTER 14

*F*areed and Salma had a peaceful night. They had set the ball in motion and now left it to divine providence to furnish the answers and show the direction. On the drive back home, they had even conveyed the situation to Asif. He had been curious about the nature of their trip to the hospital and enquired about the gentleman, Mr Khanna, who had looked at him so intently during their brief interaction.

So his parents decided to take him into confidence. Asif was taken aback initially. He now realised the cause of his father's dark moods and irritable behaviour. And he had thought it was all about him!

Well, it was his accident and the need for a probable blood transfusion that had kick-started the whole process. He felt guilty that his parents were going through a harrowing time, and he was not even aware of it. He had to be strong for them now. He hid his confusion and asked them if Ameena was aware of the happenings. 'No, until something definite is established, there is no need to trouble her,' said his dad.

Fareed now had to play the waiting game patiently. He had submitted his and Salma's samples to the hospital. It was now the responsibility of the hospital to get samples from the Khanna family and match the data.

The call came sooner than expected. And surprisingly, it was not from the hospital. It was direct from Mr Khanna.

After intense discussions, the Khannas decided to submit their blood samples to the hospital. There had been a polite request from the hospital director, Dr Gita, herself, to help them get to the bottom of the matter. The Khannas were well within their rights to refuse, and no one could coerce them into doing so. But they did it anyway because it was the right thing to do.

One could not have uncertainty gnawing at you. A wrong had to be set right, even if it meant losing a precious part of you, the vital part that kept your heart ticking, thought Anil. He recounted the lines of a popular poem.

> *If you love something, let it go,*
> *If it comes back, it is yours for ever,*
> *If it does not,*
> *It was not yours in any case.*

So Anil not only submitted samples to the hospital in question but also a second set to a private lab in town. He had to be doubly sure. He could not let another lab error or ambiguous result mess up his life. Eventually, the results from the private lab came earlier. It was confirmed that Asha's DNA did not match his or Seema's. Well, he had no way of knowing if it matched the Khans. But under the circumstances, it was the most logical conclusion.

The results had to be conveyed to all concerned. It had to be conveyed slowly and gently to minimise the havoc it was bound to cause, not only in the lives of the young girls, but also in their families. The reverberations would be felt in the extended families too. Mr Khanna reached for the phone. He knew where the first call would have to go.

If Mr Fareed was surprised to get a call from Mr Khanna, he did not show it. After polite enquiries about each other's health and well-being, they got down to brass tacks. Mr Khanna gave it to him direct.

'Our private lab results have just come in. My daughter's DNA does not match ours.'

There was a long silence at the other end. And then unexpectedly Fareed Khan said, 'I am so sorry.'

Anil was taken aback. His nerves had been steeled for a tone of exultation or at least an 'I told you' attitude. But Mr Fareed sounded genuinely sympathetic. He too had gone through the trauma a month earlier and could understand the pain and bewilderment Anil was going through.

Sensing his empathy, Anil confided sooner than he had wished to.

'My daughter Asha has an uncanny resemblance to Asif.'

It took some time for Fareed to digest this info. So that was why Anil had been staring surprisedly at Asif that day. And that was why he was making this call without waiting for the official hospital lab results. There seemed to be some light at the end of the tunnel finally. Dimly, he heard Anil asking him a question.

'And what is your daughter like?'

'She is the light of my life,' replied Fareed quietly. 'The laughter in our house. She is always cheerful and puts a smile on our faces even in the most trying circumstances,' he added.

'That is like my elder daughter, Nisha,' confided Anil.

They decided the families must meet before informing the young ones. The kids would at least know the other family before being told the real relation. It might somehow help to alleviate the fear and confusion when they were eventually informed they had been born into another family. A prior acquaintance with the biological family with no pre-conceived notions would cause less apprehension on learning the truth and probably help them bond faster. The other unspoken advantage was that the parents could be on their best behaviour.

Thus, Anil casually mentioned to his family that the following Sunday, a classmate was coming to town and they would meet up for dinner.

Fareed too explained to his family that they would be going on a trip the following weekend to visit an old classmate. Of course, Salma and Asif were in the know about the purpose of the trip. Ameena initially begged off, saying she would prefer to spend the holiday catching up on her college projects. But after some persuasion from her dad, she acquiesced.

Salma had noted that her daughter seemed a bit subdued nowadays. She was her usual, cheerful self, most of the time but occasionally lost deep in thought. And at times, a frown creased her brow. Salma wondered if their tension had rubbed off on her. But she didn't think so. If Ameena had any inkling of the situation, she would have confronted them head-on. Subtlety was not her style. But there was a change in her demeanour. Maybe, it had just got to do with growing up, shrugged Salma.

Asif knew what the matter with Ameena was. She was definitely sweet on Shoib. The previous weekend, when they had gone trekking, she had actually worn make-up. He sighed. Why did he let her join the earlier all-male group? It was a foursome of four male friends who enjoyed the outdoors and adventure of trekking. Rohit, Shoib, Karan, and himself had been friends since ages and bonded well. Then Karan had to leave town as his parents were transferred. Ameena had begged to join in and take Karan's place. Asif had agreed after some persuasion. She was on buddy terms with all his friends. There was never an awkward moment. She pulled her own weight and carried her own stuff. She was usually so matter-of-fact and cynical. Asif felt she did not have a romantic bone in her body. But he could be mistaken. There could be something cooking between her and Shoib. He felt responsible for her, especially as his parents had turned a blind eye to her outdoor activity as she was with her brother. In fact, it was they who put in a word for her when Asif was debating whether to let her join the group on the arduous treks.

Thus, when Salma voiced her misgivings to Asif, he felt constrained to confide his doubts to her, especially since Salma attributed Ameena's changed demeanor to having got wind of the situation at home. She enquired with Asif if he had hinted or conveyed anything about the doubtful parentage to her.

'No, Mom,' he had said indignantly. 'We had decided to inform her only after the final results came from the hospital. And besides that is your call. I wouldn't get into that.'

Then what could be the reason for her changed behaviour, wondered his mom aloud.

So Asif told her, 'I think she has a crush on my friend Shoib.'

Salma was suitably surprised. 'How do you know?' she exclaimed.

'I don't know for sure. Just a hunch.'

Now she was full of questions regarding Shoib.

'What do his parents do? Were they Sunnis or Shias? Which place did they originally come from?'

'Mom, relax,' pleaded Asif, amused. 'There could be nothing in it or at the most a mild infatuation.'

However, she insisted that he answer her questions. 'They are a broad-minded, educated family,' he said, 'and they are from the south.'

'And what languages do they speak at home?' she questioned him further. She was aware that the Kerala and Tamil Muslims spoke only the local languages. While those from Hyderabad and Karnataka spoke Urdu or Hindi like them. The Khan ancestors were from the north, somewhere near Rajasthan, but they had settled in Mumbai since two or three generations.

Asif was looking at her exasperatedly. 'Mom, don't get carried away. This is just a mild infatuation which youngsters go through.'

'But it could turn serious,' she quailed.

'Yes,' he admitted, 'but it could just fizzle away like the season. No need to get into a tizzy about it.'

'Anyway, tell me about him,' she insisted.

'Well, he is from Hyderabad, and his parents are professors in a government college.'

Salma heaved a sigh of relief. Well, at least they would be Urdu speaking. And being professors meant an educated and respectable family. Working in government service meant they would not be too-moneyed, but still well-off. Of course as Asif stated so emphatically, there could be nothing in it. So she decided to put the matter in the back burner for the present. There were other pressing matters to consider now, like the upcoming trip during the weekend to Pune.

Ameena was in a fix. For the first time in her young life, she was in a situation that she could not laugh off and could not trivialise. It had started innocuously enough. She had joined Asif's trekking group for the love of the sport. She had always been one of the guys, so no one objected to her presence, neither Asif nor his friends, Shoib and Rohit. They required a fourth partner after Karan had left, and it solved the problem of looking out for one. Things were going smoothly till now. Then Ameena realised that she was falling in love. She tried to fight it, but it was too late.

The gravity of the situation hit her when Asif was hospitalised and the weekly treks were called off. She could no longer meet his friends in a casual way. She felt the pangs of separation acutely. Going on dates was out of the question. Such things were not done in her family. In fact, falling in love was also not done. One got married off at a suitable age to a suitable person from a suitable family. Comparatively, her family was broad-minded but not that much. Ameena knew what they would say.

She was young and did not know her mind. This was just a passing infatuation. Luckily, no one was aware of it till now. Asif had questioned her mildly once, but she had laughed it off, and he had seemed satisfied. He had not raked it up again. And then there was his accident.

Actually, that was the time she had got really close. They had been unable to meet but compensated with long phone calls. It helped that her parents were at the hospital. There was no one to eavesdrop or complain about the inordinate time she spent on the phone. And the more she spoke to him, the more she realised that he was her soulmate.

The problem was how to convince her parents. They would be aghast on knowing the truth. Right now, they did not suspect a thing. Or did they? Sometimes, Ameena felt her father's eyes on her. It was an intangible feeling. But it was not one of reproach. It was one of sorrow. Or was it just her imagination? She was sure if her parents really got wind of the situation, there would be a scene. A terrible one. She was playing a dangerous game. She had fallen in love with the wrong boy, from the wrong religion. Asif too thought she was mooning about Shoib. Actually it was the other friend, Rohit, the strong, silent one whom she had fallen madly in love with.

CHAPTER 15

$\mathcal{F}$areed's car was speeding along the new expressway. The long drive to Pune was considerably more pleasurable after the completion of the 165 km highway. Salma was beside him while Ameena and Asif sat in the backseat. It had been a long time since the four of them had gone on a trip. Once the kids had joined college, they were tied up in many other activities. Their differing schedules made it difficult to organise a family outing. And the kids too seemed to prefer to spend the time with their friends. He recollected the old days when they were younger. They used to plead with him to take them to a park or picnic for the weekends. Many a time, he had to beg off citing office commitments. Now they were happy if their parents just left them alone!

Fareed was aware of the trekking trips Asif went with his friends during the weekends. He knew Ameena too had joined them recently and did not object as she would be under the watchful eye of Asif.

The car slowed down as it approached the town. They exited the highway and joined the bustling traffic of the town. It had grown exponentially since Fareed had last come here. Fareed had done a six-month internship here after his graduation, more than two decades ago. He was not even married then. It had been a nice, quiet town at that time. There were not many avenues for entertainment or nightlife if one enjoyed those things. Subsequently, he had gone on business trips a couple of times, but he had been busy in meetings then and not seen much of the city. Now, it was bustling with activity. He decided to take his family to his favourite haunt of earlier days. It was a huge garden with bushes cut and shaped to resemble animals. It mimicked the Hanging Gardens of Mumbai. This time, Fareed was surprised to see stalls with games for kids and adults alike. There was a bowling alley, a refreshment centre, and even an open-air theatre nearby. Enough activities to keep them occupied till they joined the Khannas for dinner at a newly opened Chinese restaurant.

The Khannas were getting ready to leave for dinner. They often did go out for a family dinner to a restaurant on the weekend as it was the cook's day off. Today, they were going for the first time to the swanky new Chinese restaurant which had recently opened up. And they were going to be joined by a childhood friend of their dad. Nisha had tried to excuse herself as it was a co-worker's birthday party. But Anil had insisted that she come along with them. She finally agreed with bad grace. She could not understand why she had to miss her friend's party to entertain her dad's friend. Life was so unfair.

So there were mutterings of discontent in the car as it sped towards the restaurant. On arrival, the beauty of the restaurant quelled her annoyance. They were led to their table in a spacious lawn by a gracious hostess. As the waiter approached to take the order, Anil indicated that they were expecting friends. The waiter nodded and withdrew. The girls wandered off to watch a waterfall. The cascading waters created ripples at the bottom and with the play of lights had a magical effect. They were so engrossed they did not notice the arrival of guests. When they turned to go back, they saw their parents greeting the guests cordially. As they walked towards the table, Asha had an intangible feeling that she was the cynosure of all the eyes.

Introductions were made. She got a warm handshake from her dad's friend and a hug from his wife. Their son looked at her curiously, and their daughter was in an animated conversation with her mom.

As they prepared to sit down, Salma smiled at Asha and indicated a chair beside her. Asha obliged and sat next to her. Their daughter was already seated next to her mom.

As the conversation wore on, Nisha had the weirdest feeling. It was as though she was not present at the table. The guest couple were engrossed with Asha and directing all their questions at her. Her parents were busy chatting to their daughter, who was replying politely to them. Their son Asif was sitting quietly but was keenly following the conversation between his parents and Asha.

No one made an effort to converse with Nisha. Well, she did not really even want to come to this get-together, she thought. Maybe her reluctance to come had subconsciously reflected in her attitude. She was probably sending out sparks of hostility.

As the evening wore on, she grew wearier. She should have insisted and gone to her friend's birthday party. Now, she was stuck with this boring group. The long-drawn-out dinner was finally drawing to a close. Nisha refused the dessert. She had her figure to think about and anything to end the evening early. However, the rest of the group ordered dessert and lingered over it too. Nisha was thoroughly exasperated. Finally, the waiter arrived with the bill, which her dad promptly paid by credit card.

It was time now for goodbyes. The Khans insisted that the Khannas too come to their place for dinner soon. Fat chance, thought Nisha and looked aghast as her parents nodded their agreement. Soon, there were handshakes, hugs, and goodbyes. Nisha noted she got a handshake while Asha got a hug.

Things were rather quiet in the car as Fareed drove back from the dinner. It was Asif who broke the silence. 'So how did you like the Khannas?' He asked Ameena casually.

'A nice family,' she said, 'and Aunty was so very pleasant. But, boy, was she curious? She wanted to know what I like and dislike and what I am studying and even my grades.'

'I suppose that is because they have a daughter of your age, so they were probably comparing notes,' said Asif.

'Yeah, they did mention their younger daughter too just turned eighteen.'

'And what did you think of her?'

'Well, she hardly spoke to me,' said Ameena. 'She must be quite snooty. At least, her sister tried to make conversation with me. If her mom wasn't monopolising my time, I could probably have hit it off with her.'

Fareed and Salma exchanged glances. This was an aspect they had not thought of. New sibling relationships too would have to be taken into account.

The Khanna car was brimming with resentment and reproach. Nisha was angry, and she was vocal about it. 'I so much wanted to go to my friend's party. But you guys had to drag me here.'

'Sometimes, one had to observe social formalities,' said her dad mildly.

'I don't force you to sit around when I meet my friends,' she told her dad sharply. 'In fact, we'd love to be left alone.'

'Nisha,' remonstrated her mom, 'don't speak to your dad like that.'

Thereafter, the car was filled with sullen silence. Asha was amused. It was rare for Nisha to lose her cool and sulk. And when it happened, it lasted for a couple of days at least before her sunny nature took over. Asha, in contrast, had quite enjoyed the evening. She loved Chinese food and liked the ambience of the restaurant. And the guests too were nice. They really seemed to take an interest in her. They asked about her likes, dislikes, and enquired about her hobbies and other interests. Their son had sat quietly but seemed to be following the conversation. At times, he seemed to have an amused air. Her parents were having an animated conversation with their daughter, which Nisha could have joined in, thought Asha.

CHAPTER 16

*A*sha had a long dreamless sleep. She woke up calm and refreshed. She dressed and left for college. She had a long strenuous day at college. Assignments had to be submitted, and some lecture notes to be exchanged. She came back exhausted but cheerful. She found Nisha talking animatedly on the phone to her friend, discussing the birthday party she had missed. Her sunny disposition seemed to have returned. Asha had her wash and tiptoed to the kitchen to check out the dinner menu. Her mom was putting the finishing touches to the dinner. Asha appreciatively noted the paneer matar and bhindi masala, being set on the table.

'I am famished,' she declared.

Her mom smiled. 'Bring your sister down, and both of you can have your dinner,' she said. 'Dad will be late today, so no point waiting for him.' Nisha came down with the mobile glued to her ear. Her mother frowned. 'No talking while eating,' she remonstrated.

'I thought mealtimes were for conversation,' replied Nisha.

'Talk to those at the table,' replied her mom evenly.

'Hey, no one spoke to me yesterday,' pointed out Nisha. 'You were engrossed with their daughter, and they were mesmerised with Asha,' she added airily.

Asha grinned. Nisha had not totally forgotten yesterday's outing.

Asha glanced at her mom and was surprised to see a strained expression on her face.

Nisha, oblivious to her mom's mood, was watching Asha's heaped plate. 'It is so nice you can tuck in and not pile on the pounds,' she commented.

'Yeah, I guess I have a high metabolic rate,' said Asha.

'I noticed yesterday their son too was eating with gusto but is still thin and wiry like you.'

'Is it?' asked Asha, munching away hungrily.

'Yeah. In fact, he looked a lot like you. He could be easily mistaken for your brother.'

'Nisha,' said her mother sharply, 'finish your meal. Don't make idle conversation.'

Both the girls looked at their mother, surprised at her sudden sharp tone. Her face was a tight mask.

'Now, I can't talk even at the table,' grumbled Nisha in an aggrieved tone.

Asha continued staring at her mom. Something stirred in her. She had consciously put the events of the previous month at the back of her mind. By mutual agreement, they had decided to wait for the hospital lab reports before discussing the matter further. She looked down blankly at her food. Suddenly, she had lost her appetite. Nisha was munching away, oblivious to the tension in the room.

As soon as she could, Asha escaped to her room. Her head was throbbing. When Nisha came to bid her goodnight, she found her fast asleep. But sleep did not come easily to Asha. She tossed and turned. She tried to make sense of Nisha's casual observation. It there was any truth in her casual remarks, then the Khan family would probably be the one with the exchanged baby. That couple would be her biological parents, and the boy with the amused air, keenly following the conversation, would be her brother. It also meant that unlike Nisha, he was aware of the situation.

Asha tried to recollect their daughter. They had just exchanged a casual greeting, and since she was seated at the far end of the table, there was no further interaction between them. Their daughter had been busy chatting with her parents, answering their queries politely.

Asha instinctively knew she was clueless about the issue. The only reason Asha was in the know was because she had inadvertently stumbled in on a phone conversation. Her parents too would never have told her, till it was inevitable, and they had checked the facts and got 100 per cent proof. Parents too could be devious, thought Asha.

Their son knew because he too probably stumbled on to the secret. Or maybe the parents decided to confide in their eldest child. He did look rather wise and mature for his age. But why didn't her dad inform her if the lab tests confirmed anything?

Asha rose from the bed when the first rays of sunlight peeped into her room. Her dad was an early riser and used the solitude of the early hours to read the newspaper in peace. Well, today he would be disturbed, she thought grimly. She walked quietly into the veranda, where he was sipping his tea while reading the newspaper. He was surprised to see her up so early. Though he had been expecting a confrontation after Seema had told him about the turn of the dinner conversation.

'Good morning,' he greeted her calmly. 'You are up pretty early today.'

'Well, I did not sleep whole night,' she replied shortly.

'Oh,' he said, as he put down the paper.

'Dad, why didn't you tell me the hospital lab results had come out?'

'They have not come yet,' he said mildly. She looked at him in disbelief. 'I had sent some samples to a private lab here too. I only got their result, but they are not reliable.'

'And what did their results indicate?'

'Well, this lab is not specialised in this field, so the results cannot be relied on. They would not stand up in a court of law.'

'But still what did it say?'

'They did find some discrepancy,' he said quietly.

He looked anxiously at her shocked expression. The blood had drained from her face.

'But I am still waiting for the official lab tests from the hospital,' he said lamely. 'Only after that was confirmed, I wanted to convey it to you.'

'But you have conveyed it to the other family,' she said accusingly.

He looked downcast, almost guiltily.

'When I saw their son at the hospital, I was struck by his similarity with you. It seemed evident you were siblings.'

No wonder he looked as though he had seen a ghost, thought Asha. She remembered seeing him with a blank expression as she had stepped out of the auto on that fateful day. Things had moved fast since then. She had actually met her birth parents. The official results were now just a formality. The delay conveniently gave the parents some time to groom them, to mentally prepare them and soften the impact of the news. Well, Asha knew now. The other girl was oblivious to the drama that was to unfold in her life soon. As soon as an innocuous report was received from the lab.

Asha walked back to her room in a daze. She wondered what that girl's reaction would be. Well, that girl had already met her birth parents in a conducive atmosphere. She would have formed a favourable opinion of them with the care they lavished on her that day. Poor, unsuspecting girl, chatting away gaily, thought Asha. She could not even recollect her name. She realised only Nisha and that girl were out of the loop now. The news would impact Nisha too even though she was not directly involved. She would get a new sister. And I a new brother, realised Asha with a start. As she examined her feelings, she decided that she quite liked the thought of having a brother.

CHAPTER 17

$\mathcal{F}$areed and Salma had intense discussions regarding when and how to convey the situation to their daughter. Fareed was all for waiting till the official lab results were in hand, before broaching the topic with Ameena. But Salma reasoned with him. The matter was an open and shut case. Many of them were aware of it now. Before Ameena stumbled on it herself or overheard from someone else, it was better to sit her down and convey it to her gently.

'It is just a matter of a few days more,' Fareed pleaded with Salma. He was trying to put off the inevitable. He could not bear to see the hurt and pain in her face. However, Salma's argument too carried merit. Finally, they decided to tell her the following weekend. Sunday was the time when all of them would be at home and relaxed. Fareed made a discreet call to the hospital and was told that the results would be ready at the latest by Monday. Sunday would be as good a time as any other, he decided.

Ameena had been looking forward to the weekly Saturday treks with Asif and his friends. When it rained on Friday, she was filled with apprehension. If the downpour continued to the next day, the trek would have to be called off. It would then be another week before she could meet Rohit. Luckily, Saturday was bright and sunny. Ameena rose early, gleefully noted the favourable weather, and was dressed before Asif. He grinned when he saw her.

'Someone seems to have made a deal with the Rain God,' he commented.

'Yes, I told him my couch potato brother needs his exercise,' she replied. She knew he was referring to her enthusiasm to meet Shoib. He would be shocked when he learnt the truth. And her parents would be terribly hurt. She wondered how long she could keep the secret. Only Shoib knew the real situation, and he played along sportingly. But Ameena knew, sooner or later, she would have to reveal the truth to her family, before they found out themselves.

The trek was exhausting but enjoyable. There was an uncommonly large crowd today. People had come outdoors to enjoy the sunshine after two days of rain. Shoib sportingly walked ahead with Asif, who thought it was he who was setting the brisk pace. If it was his intention to separate the two love birds, he had succeeded admirably, he thought.

Ameena lagged behind with Rohit. She could conveniently have a conversation with him without being overheard by Asif. They discussed the reaction of their respective families on getting to know that they were a couple. Rohit admitted that it would be an uphill task to convince his parents. They were not too conservative but would balk at the thought of someone from another religion. They expected him to marry within the same community. They would probably accept an inter-caste one too. But cutting across religious lines would be too shocking for them. It would be a daunting task to convince them to accept her as a daughter in law. Ameena too admitted it was the same with her family. Rohit declared that he would stand by her in spite of stiff opposition from his family. The only concession he asked was that she should wait till he completed his studies and landed a job. That was less than a year away. They would have to lie low till then. Ameena frowned at the thought of continuing the subterfuge for a year. She was not comfortable at the thought of deceiving her parents. She had always been open with her parents. She would love to tell them about this and get it over with. But it was probably wise to wait till the situation was more conducive.

Asif and Shoib had reached the end of the summit and were waiting for them. Asif noted the frown on Ameena's face and smiled. Ah, she is not happy I walked off with her beau, he thought. He owed it to his parents to see that the casual friendship with his friend did not develop into something serious. It would be easy to quash a budding romance if it was still in the puppy phase.

As the four of them made their way down, after conquering the summit, a strange silence enveloped them. Usually, there was a light banter. Asif felt a bit guilty. 'Race you to the bottom,' he said and sprinted off. He fully expected Rohit to comply and Shoib to hang back. Instead, Shoib sportingly took up the challenge and raced with him while Rohit and Ameena trekked down at a casual pace. Shoib was trying to deflect suspicion in case their weekly treks became a casualty, decided Asif. It had begun to drizzle lightly and the laggards Rohit and Ameena quickened their pace. They had reached the car just before the downpour began. Somehow, the mood in the car was jolly as they sipped their tea. It was exhilarating to watch the rain beating outside while they were comfortably ensconced inside the car. They munched the snacks, thoughtfully brought by Ameena, and indulged in the usual light-hearted banter.

They reached home, flushed and happy. 'Had a good time?' asked Fareed as they entered.

'Superb,' replied Asif. But Fareed was watching Ameena. She seemed so happy and carefree, he thought. And all that would change tomorrow, when the mix-up regarding her birth was revealed to her. He wondered again for the umpteenth time whether he should postpone it by a few more days. But then as Salma had pointed out, it risked her getting to know of it through another source.

Ameena was aware of her dad looking at her in concern. She felt a pang of guilty. Did he see through her deceit? She tried to give a nonchalant smile. He was still frowning. His brow was creased in furrows. Ameena knew something was up. He had somehow got wind of the situation. But instead of firing her as expected, he was saddened. The calm before the storm, she thought. The discomfort showed in her face.

As soon as she could, she escaped to her room. But not before her dad had conveyed that the next day there were some important family matters to discuss.

After a fitful sleep, Ameena got up with a sense of foreboding. She would have to face the music today. The storm would have been brewing in the night and would erupt in the morning. She took her own sweet time for her morning ablutions. It was like she was unwilling to face the day. She delayed as far as it was possible to do so. She then gingerly poked her head out of the room. The appetising smell of breakfast wafted in the air. Her favourite kheema paratha was being made today. Her dad and Asif were already at the table. She went and joined them. Her mother piled her plate with parathas.

Sunday morning was the only time the family had breakfast together. And it was an elaborate one. Today was no different. But there was something in the air. Ameena felt her parents exchanging covert glances. Her sense of foreboding returned. Did they know? How could they? Even Asif didn't know. And even if he did, he would have accosted her first. He owed her that much. And by nature, he was not a sneak. To be fair to him, he always sided with her.

As her mother cleared the table, she headed for the sitting room and picked up the newspaper. She was not a regular newspaper reader, but the Sunday paper was an exception. She went through the features and articles rather than the news. She was in the midst of the paper when she realised her parents too had entered and were sitting patiently in the room.

Fareed cleared his throat. 'Beta, we have something to discuss with you,' he said.

She put down her newspaper with trepidation. So this was it. She had been trying to convince herself, that the tension she felt during breakfast was her imagination. But it was not to be so. Guilt and fear flooded her senses. She lowered her face to hide her feelings. She steeled herself to hear an accusing tone. But surprisingly, her father continued in a gentle tone.

'We will always love you come what may. Life has many surprises in store. Some are good, and some not so good. But one must accept the inevitability of God's will.' Ameena was confused. What was he trying to say? She looked at her mom. Her face was inscrutable. She just reached out and held Ameena's arm. Wild thoughts raced through Ameena's mind. What were they trying to convey? Was it a subtle preclude to making her accept a marriage proposal? Maybe after getting wind of the situation, they decided to quickly and quietly make her tie the knot into a suitable family. Through a daze, she heard her dad say, 'You will always be our daughter. And this will always be your home.'

Yeah, she knew that. It was a polite way of pointing out that after marriage, it was not really her house. A married daughter was a guest in her parents' house. Her parents did not intend to face the situation head-on. She was filled with apprehension. They were not accusing her of deceit. They were not remonstrating with her. They were just getting rid of her. She felt like a sacrificial lamb at the altar.

She bit her lip to prevent the tears rolling down her face. She looked up and was surprised to see her father's eyes full of tears. His voice was choked with emotion, and he nodded to Salma, 'You tell her.'

And her mother did. Ameena listened incredulously. Nothing had prepared her for these revelations. A story about mix-up of babies at the maternity home. Realisation striking only when the blood transfusions were deemed to be incompatible.

The tears that had welled up earlier now flowed freely. Umpteen questions dogged her mind. The confusion showed on her face. Her mother hugged her tightly. If all this was true, she was not her mother. And her dad was not her father. And Asif? Well, a brother was always a brother. Where was he now? Did he know? Her mother nodded. He knew.

And then, who were her biological parents? Had they been traced? Were they known? Gently, her mother told her. Ameena was shocked. The family they had met the previous weekend were her birth parents! The truth was being revealed in layers. It was like the peeling of the layers of an onion, one by one. It was inevitable that tears flowed with the unpeeling of layers of an onion.

A sobbing Ameena tried to collect her thoughts. She remembered the couple and how gracious they were to her. She had been so honoured by the attention they had bestowed on her. Their elder daughter had been seated opposite her and was having a petulant expression on her face, probably at being ignored in the conversation. Ameena had only a vague recollection of their younger daughter. She was seated at the far end of the table. And yes, she was engrossed with her parents.

It was a good plan both the parents had hatched, meeting the biological, unsuspecting offspring in a neutral setting. They had the advantage of prior knowledge. They could direct the conversation smoothly. Ameena slowly realised that the entire conversation was all about her. She had not asked them anything. She did not even know their names, where they lived or what they did for a living.

Vaguely she recollected that her dad had said they would be meeting his classmate, the Khanna family. So that meant they were Hindus. Another thought crept up unbidden. If she was the genetic offspring of a Hindu family, opposition to her marriage with Rohit would be quelled. His family too would probably tone down their objection.

Through the mayhem, Ameena could see a silver lining. She had been fretting before the discussion that the outcome was to drive a wedge between her and Rohit. Inadvertently, the unexpected and shocking revelation had paved the way for them. Her parents' uneasiness and covert looks since past few days were not due to the knowledge of her secret. They had no inkling of that at all. Their tension was due to the burden of their own big secret, of which Ameena too had absolutely no inkling till now. Well, now she knew. She had been so dreading the discussion. The situation had now taken such an unexpected turn. If her feelings were not so raw, she would have smiled. She gave a deep sigh. She was much calmer now. She went to her room and had a long nap. It was dark when she awoke. Her head was still heavy and throat sore with sobs. Her mom came in with hot soup. She drank it quietly and fell asleep till morning.

CHAPTER 18

*I*t was the Monday morning after the Sunday revelation. The Khan household was subdued. The shrieking of the telephone shattered the silence. Fareed gingerly picked up the phone. As expected, it was from the nursing home. It was the day when the official lab results from the hospital was scheduled to be conveyed to them. The caller identified herself as Dr Gita. In measured tones, she told him the DNA sequence revealed that the exchange of babies had in fact taken place. Asha was their genetic daughter, and Ameena belonged to the Khannas. Fareed listened stoically. The result had been a foregone conclusion. Now that it was officially confirmed, decisions had to be taken. Myriad thoughts crossed his mind. Through a daze, he realised the voice at the other end of the line was still speaking softly. He forced himself to listen. It was the doctor apologising for the mistake that had occurred in the nursing home and enquiring if there was anything she could do to help settle matters. She assured him that the events that occurred eighteen years ago would be investigated and the staff members involved in the mix-up would be identified and reprimanded. The unspoken question was, would they press charges? Did they intend to sue the hospital? Fareed shook his head imperceptibly. He was not interested in pursuing the Why's and How's of the mix-up. It had happened a long time ago. The staff members would be retired or deceased. He had gone over the episode so many times in his mind the past one month. He realised it was a mix-up that had occurred at the level of the nurses and ayahs. Sometimes, even with the best of precautions, things happened. He did not want to dwell on that aspect anymore. He had other issues to face, other battles to fight, which concerned the future. Making heads roll for an inadvertent mistake that occurred way back in the past would not help smoothen the way for the present or future.

In a steady voice, he interrupted the doctor, 'I have no intention of pursuing an investigation into the incident.' He heard an audible sigh of relief. 'The hospital is welcome to investigate the matter, not to apportion blame, but to instil measures so that such incidents are not repeated in the future,' he continued.

Dr Gita listened quietly and said, 'I appreciate your stand. We are grateful to you for your understanding. Let me assure you that this is the only case of this nature that has occurred in this hospital in the nearly thirty years I have been here. Nevertheless, we will investigate the events leading to this colossal blunder so that it does not occur again.'

Fareed listened to her explanation and expressed his appreciation to her for promptly acknowledging the mistake and not making an attempt at cover-up.

Gita took a deep breath after her conversation with Fareed. She now had to ring up Mr Khanna. He took the news calmly. It was as if they had already known, thought Dr Gita. Maybe they had confirmed it at a private lab testing facility. If a mistake had to occur, it could not have happened to a nicer set of patients, thought Dr Gita ruefully. Both were fine gentlemen. In a way, she did cater to the educated middle class. But one could find rabble rousers in all strata of society.

Dr Gita grew thoughtful. This incident, if made public, would give undeserved notoriety to the nursing home she had built up so lovingly. It had been her life, even more so after her divorce. As far as she knew, no such incident had occurred in the nearly thirty years she had been there. But even one mistake of this nature is one too many, she decided. It was a blemish on her perfect record. The notoriety of the exchanged babies would mar the reputation of the clinic. She had been in talks with a young couple, both doctors, who wished to take over the clinic. Dr Gita was well past sixty now. She had wished to retire since a couple of years. But she had not found anyone suitable to pass on the responsibility of the nursing home that she had nurtured for so long. And then she was approached by this couple who had just returned from a stint abroad. Their kids were on the verge of joining colleges in India. Instead of just packing off the kids to stay in hostels, the full family decided to relocate. This new generation of expats who returned from foreign lands were called repats, a new term coined by an intrepid newspaper columnist. Repats referred those who returned to their homeland after a stint abroad. They had made adequate money and wished to live on their terms. They had enthusiasm and fresh ideas. Gita knew she could trust this couple with the clinic.

It was just a few years ago that Gita celebrated twenty-five years of taking over the clinic. The staff had insisted that she throw a party. The hospital was decorated with flowers and lights. Even the patients had a smile on their face as they were given treats. Vinod had come down from the city. Venkat too had sent his felicitations. He was still working in the city in a corporate hospital and had become the chief administrator. He had settled into a life of domestic bliss. His wife did not work since marriage and she kept home. Dr Gita had seen them once only, on the occasion of Vinod's wedding a decade ago. They had seemed happy, and Gita did not grudge them their happiness. Vinod's marriage to a colleague was met with approval by both his parents. The girl was a beautiful, smart young woman, who had done her MBA along with Vinod. Dr Gita was now blessed with two grandkids. Vinod insisted she visit them more often so that the kids benefit from her company. Nothing made Gita happier than the time spent with her grandchildren. But the responsibilities of the nursing home precluded too many trips. With age catching up, she had decided it was time to take things easy and pass on her nursing home to safe hands. By a stroke of luck, she had found the prefect couple. But first she had to resolve the matter which had cropped up recently, so she could hand over a clean slate to the new owners. Once again, she thanked her stars that the one mistake that had occurred happened to a pair of understanding families. There would be no public outcry or mudslinging involved. She could now retire in peace and hand over the clinic to a fresh pair of hands.

Anil Khanna took the call from Dr Gita stoically. The official confirmation ended one chapter of the situation. The next chapter would start now. They had to make decisions regarding the girls' future and how to go ahead.

It was time to make another call to Fareed.

Anil and Fareed agreed that for the time being, the girls would remain in the households they had been raised in. They had two more years of college to complete. They could slowly get to know the biological family over this period and meet the extended family members too. Technically, they were adults now, but a two-year leeway to make decisions for their future seemed a good idea.

Fareed was in total agreement to Anil's suggestion that the girls continue to stay in the household they had been raised. They were too young to be uprooted now. The unanswered question was the matter of religion. Fareed knew if Asha had to gain acceptance into his extended family, she would have to accept the religion of her birth parents. He balked at the thought of explaining the matter to his relatives. His brother Kabir and sister Tasneem would have to be informed about the new addition to the family. Kabir's wife came from a family of devout Muslims, and she observed the purdah. Her daughters too observed purdah when they came of age, and she always looked askance at Ameena's casual ways.

Anil and Seema were loath to lose Asha even after her graduation. But thoughts of Ameena kept cropping up in their minds. Was she happy in that household? Seema was determined to bring Ameena into her household. She got an opportunity during the summer holidays. She suggested to Fareed that he send over Ameena so that she could get to know her sister Nisha whom she resembled. She explained that Asha had extra classes and fieldwork during the summer hols, so she would be unable to reciprocate.

Fareed agreed after discussion with his wife and daughter. Salma had been waiting for an opportunity to get Asha into her home. But she did not want to renege on the deal made by her husband. Since the initial suggestion came from the Khannas, she could now play her hand. She was disappointed that Fareed meekly accepted their excuse for not sending Asha. She entreated with him to insist that they send Asha, but he resisted her pleas. 'She will come when she is ready,' he said.

Ameena seemed pleased to go and meet her biological family. Her parent were unaware of the undercurrents in her desire to forge a relationship with her biological family.

Ameena's expected arrival put the Khanna household in a tizzy. The guest bedroom was spring cleaned and readied for her arrival. To curious neighbours, it was decided to explain her presence as a friend of the girls. Seema could not contain her excitement. Till now, Seema had only confided in her elder sister, Rekha. Her other sibling, the eldest brother, was abroad with his family. He made infrequent visits to India. Rekha too was all agog at the thought of meeting Ameena. She was a jolly, bubbly person who spoke nineteen to the dozen. She was very fond of her younger sister's daughters as she had two sons. Both had left home for college. The elder one had passed out from a Regional Engineering College and was doing a postgraduate course in USA. The younger one had gone directly after his schooling on a scholarship abroad. So Rekha and her husband faced the prospect of an empty nest at an early age. The frequency of their visits to Seema's household increased with the departure of their sons to distant shores.

It was Anil's suggestion not to overwhelm Ameena on her arrival. Give her space, he admonished Seema. They should not frighten her away with too many queries. That could come later. Seema nodded her agreement.

Thus, Ameena found a restrained welcome when she arrived on a Saturday evening. The family had dinner together, and it was as if a dear but distant relative had come visiting. Conversation was restricted to the news of the day and the latest movies being screened. As Ameena retired to her room, she marvelled at the dignity of her biological family. They had made her feel welcome without smothering her.

On Sunday, Rekha came to spend the day. She too was curious to meet her new niece. She gave Ameena a warm hug and observed her minutely. Either she had not been told to be discreet or it had fallen to deaf ears. At the outset, she told Ameena that she was her aunt and could be addressed as Rekha maasi. 'And I will call you Meena,' she declared. There was a sudden silence in the room. Anil glanced at Seema. Hadn't she told her sister to hold her tongue? Rekha continued with her chatter unaware of the disapproving looks.

After dinner, Seema had a word with her sister. Rekha was surprised at being remonstrated. She explained that the small change in name, dropping of an alphabet, was no big deal. It would help her blend with all their relations. Besides, she did not seem to mind, pointed out Rekha to Seema.

That was true. Ameena did not get offended. In fact in the privacy of her room, she rolled the new name around her tongue. Just a missing alphabet, but it sounded so different. And it rhymed so well. Rohit and Meena sounded so good together. A perfect match. Hopefully, others too would think so. She slept with a contended smile on her face.

Ameena grew to the house and family. However, she missed the daily banter with Asif. Here everybody was polite to a fault. It was the first time she was with the species called sister. She was not sure whether it was better than having a brother. She felt a coldness from Asha. But she took a shine to Nisha, and the feeling was mutual.

CHAPTER 19

$\mathcal{N}$isha was informed about the situation after the official results from the hospital had been declared. She was flabbergasted. With hindsight, the events during the Chinese dinner of the previous month with her dad's so-called classmate made sense. No wonder they were all so engrossed with each other's daughters. No wonder Asif had an amused smile on his face. With a start, Nisha realised that she was the last one in the group to be made aware of the mix-up. She had been the only one out of the loop since the past one month. She did not know whether to be offended by that. She was not directly involved, her parents explained to her gently, so they wished to spare her the details till it was confirmed. As the sequence of events that led to the exchange of babies were explained to Nisha, she gulped. Slowly, she realised that although she was not directly involved, she had played a pivotal part at the inception.

She dimly recalled being excited about getting a baby sister. Her mother had explained away her expanding tummy, as a baby doll for Nisha to play with. Little Nisha could not wait for the baby to arrive. She remembered the excitement of going to the hospital and seeing the baby for the first time. Rest was a blur. Did she really pick up the baby and walk out to the corridor? Did she wail when the nurse took away the baby from her? Was the wail due to a premonition of the events which would occur? At that tiny age, she had played a crucial role in the drama.

That fact restrained her from volubly expressing her resentment at being the last to be informed. She was the one who caused all this mayhem, she thought guiltily. With of course a little help from the hospital staff. They were efficient, she knew, but had probably got so used to the daily routine of the job that their senses had been dulled. There was no one to apportion the blame. It had happened. One could look at the bright side, thought Nisha. She had another younger sister.

Thus, Nisha went out of the way to be friendly to Ameena. Ameena too warmed to her. Bantering with her brother was one thing. But being able to confide in a sister was another. In no time, the matter of Rohit was divulged to Nisha. Nisha was sympathetic to her cause. She resolved to help smoothen the matter for her. It was the least she could do. She had unknowingly, as a small child, been instrumental in causing a crisis in Ameena's life. Now, it was her turn to help resolve one.

Anil and Seema were surprised and delighted to see the easy camaraderie that had sprung up between Nisha and Ameena. 'After all, they are blood sisters,' declared Rekha helpfully. They glared at her. 'She too calls her Meena,' she added unconcernedly. Anil walked out of the room. His sister-in-law was irrepressible, he thought. He also noted that Asha and Meena never spent much time with each other. Oops, he too had called her Meena. It seemed so appropriate, Nisha and Meena. The names rhymed and so did the girls. He wondered idly what they were discussing and chatting about during the long hours they spent together. Catching up on lost time, he thought amusedly. He would have been very surprised if he had known. He did not have to wait long.

Nisha's favourite aunt, Rekha, unwittingly provided an opportunity for Nisha to raise the topic of Ameena's love interest. Rekha had always been concerned about Nisha's impending marriage. She reminded Seema that Nisha was at the right age and that waiting longer for a groom would not help matters. 'Wait a little longer, and suitable proposals will dry up,' she warned. Seema nodded dutifully in agreement but did not quicken the pace for the search of a groom. She was aware that nowadays many marriages were fixed on Internet sites like Shaadi.com, etc. but did not feel the need to go into that right now. It would happen when it had to happen, she thought philosophically.

And then Rekha herself proposed a match. Her husband's cousin, Kavita, was looking for a bride for her son. The son was a computer engineer, working in a software company in USA. He was in India for the renewal of his H1B visa. His parents planned to kill two birds with one stone and were discreetly enquiring among family and friends about a suitable girl for him. Rekha's ears perked up on hearing about the young man. She sounded Seema about the possibility of the alliance.

Thus, it was that Anil and Seema conveyed to Nisha about the marriage proposal. Photographs were exchanged, and even before the visit of the boy and his family, the youngsters had chatted on the net and checked each other out. They seemed to like what they saw, and a meeting was arranged for the following weekend.

The boy, Akshay, and his parents flew down from Delhi to see the girl. It was Nisha's turn to dress up in finery, and she had both Ameena and Asha to fuss over her. Playing out the role of a coy bride was not really her forte, but she did a commendable job. His parents were suitably impressed. Both the families approved of the match much to Rekha's delight.

The boy's mother suggested an engagement ceremony before the boy returned to the States. That was just a couple of weeks away, and Seema despaired of organising a function in such a short span. However, Rekha urged her to comply.

'We can have a small engagement ceremony with just immediate family before the boy leaves,' she suggested to Seema. 'That way they are both spoken for and will eliminate the uncertainty. We can have a grand ceremony and umpteen functions for the wedding next year.'

Seema had to agree. Nisha was not getting any younger. And when she had agreed to the proposal, it was better to finalise it now. Asha too would be finishing her college in a year's time and would be next in line. And then she thought about Ameena. She wondered if she and Anil would be allowed to play a role in her wedding. It troubled her that Ameena might not get a chance to view the groom or have a say in the decision of her wedding. She voiced her misgivings to Anil.

'It's a long time before Asha or Ameena has to think of marriage,' said Anil. 'They are still very young. The Khans are a modern and broad-minded family. Fareed will not compel his daughter to do anything she does not want to,' he reassured Seema. But he too was worried. Thus, he had a word with Nisha.

Nisha sensed the opportunity to confide in her dad. She told him how Ameena had found her life partner. They were compatible in all aspects. Anil was surprised. He had not thought Ameena was old enough for these emotions. Nisha, four years her senior, was still a babe in the woods according to him. If they had not goaded Nisha to think about marriage, she would have happily continued with her carefree days at her parental home. He had only now begun to accept that Nisha was grown up enough to think about marriage. He supposed that Ameena had an infatuation with a classmate.

Nisha had a tough time making him understand the gravity of the situation. First, she had to convince him that it was not puppy love, but something Ameena was very serious about. And then came the shocker as she told him the name of the boy. The significance was not lost on Anil. No wonder Ameena showed such enthusiasm to come to their house. Asha had shown no such inclination to go to her birth parents' house. Anil was in a dilemma. If he raked the topic with the Khan household, it would appear that he was trying to get Ameena into their fold. It could easily upset the balance of the delicate situation in which they were all placed. The veneer of civility which they had maintained during the entire unfolding of events could be wiped off in a jiffy. On the other hand, he could not abandon his biological daughter to her fate. It was a stroke of fate that had separated her from her birth parents and it was probably destined that she return to the community of her ancestors.

Seema was wholly involved in the arrangements for the engagement ceremony, which was slated for an auspicious date just ten days away. The services of a pujari had to be requisitioned, and clothes had to be bought and fitted. Near and dear relatives had to be informed. It was decided to invite only the closest relatives. The larger circle of cousins and distant relatives could come for the actual wedding. Anil's brother flew down from Delhi. He was keen to see the new addition to the family, he explained.

'The boy is excellent,' Anil assured him.

'I did not mean the boy,' said Ashutosh, his elder brother. 'I can see him anytime in Delhi. Their house at Noida is not too far away from ours. I want to see the girl, my niece.' Anil understood. Ashutosh wanted to see Meena. This would be an opportunity for Meena to meet her relatives. They debated inviting Fareed and his family to the engagement. Anil thought it was a good idea, but Seema cautioned him. They would have to give too many explanations to all the relatives. Let them face one issue at a time. Anil nodded in agreement. The issue of Ameena's romance was at the back of his mind. He did not want to be accused by her parents of encouraging her. The information would have to be conveyed to them delicately at a later time. Meanwhile, Meena could participate in the rituals of her sister's engagement and become familiar with what she would have to experience at a later date, provided her parents agreed to her nuptials with her chosen beau.

The day of the engagement saw feverish activity in the Khanna household. Since morning, there had been a steady stream of workers in and out of the house. The entrance had been bedecked with flowers, decorative fairy lights had been put up, and the services of a caterer had been requisitioned. The groom's family were staying in a nearby hotel. It included two maternal uncles with family and a paternal aunt with her daughters. The groom's sister too had come down with her husband and toddler. It was a group of more than twenty people.

Ashutosh too came down with his wife and sons. Anil and Ashutosh's only sister Deepika could not make it as she was on a foreign trip with her husband. She promised to come for the wedding and implored her brother Anil to give her adequate notice the next time. Seema had to explain to her that the short notice for the engagement was due to the fact that the boy had to return to the States.

Rekha and her husband were of course very much in the centre of things. It was they who welcomed the groom's family and entertained their relatives. The only other invitees were friends and co-workers of Nisha and of course the immediate neighbours, who had watched the girls grow from childhood to adolescence.

Nisha was decked out in all her finery. She had two bridesmaids to attend to her, Asha and Ameena. The ceremony went off smoothly. The pujari kept it short and sweet. Rings were exchanged, and gifts presented to the parents of the bride and groom. The photographer recorded it for posterity and then there was the grand repast. Meena enjoyed every bit of it. No one commented about her presence. Those who knew, knew. And those who did not assumed she was a friend of Nisha.

The day after the engagement ceremony, Nisha and Akshay went out for dinner by themselves. The entire family had gone on a picnic during the day and were resting during the evening. The sensible among them had suggested to the others to give the couple some privacy.

It was during the private dinner with Akshay that Nisha confided the story of her younger sister. It was the first time Akshay and she were having a conversation without half-a-dozen people in the room. She found he was easy to talk to. He was surprised at the information but agreed to keep it under wraps for now. 'So I have not one but two *Saalis,*' he teased.

CHAPTER 20

Asha noted the importance given to the house guest. She observed how the girl was given a prominent role in the engagement ceremony. She was being called Meena, and she did not seem to mind. Asha did not resent her presence but wondered at her enthusiasm to integrate into the family. As of present, Asha had no inclination to be part of her birth family. Luckily, they too had not made any demand or request. She watched the rapport between Nisha and Ameena. They certainly seemed to have a lot to discuss. Nisha loved to play the role of an elder sister, and now she had one more protégé. Ameena too seemed to hit it off with her blood sister.

And suddenly, Asha wished to see her brother. The the one who resembled her so much, that one look at him had made her dad realise they were siblings. Nisha too had commented on the similarity. Asha had not paid too much attention to him during the dinner. She had been monopolised by his parents. He had stayed in the background and had preferred to remain unobtrusive.

But Asha knew that it was his accident and the probable need for a blood transfusion which established the fact that Ameena was not his blood sister. It was that incident which had kick-started the process of looking for the right one. He had unwittingly played a crucial role in uncovering the issue and bringing the families together. Asha smiled at the irony. Nisha had played a role in separating the girls from the birth parents and Asif had provided the impetus to reacquaint the girls with their biological families. So both the siblings played pivotal parts in the drama. In the absence of Asif's accident, maybe they would have spent their entire lives being unaware of the exchange. Maybe, it was his blood calling out to her, mused Asha. She had always wondered how it would be to have a brother. Asha was now determined to make contact with this brother of hers.

She heard Ameena talk to him occasionally on the mobile. They seemed to share an easy rapport. The urge to meet her brother grew strong in Asha. Tentatively, one morning she dialled his mobile number. She had noted it earlier from Ameena's phone.

Asif was surprised to get a call from Asha. He knew his parents were yearning to meet her but were hesitant to make the first move. Well, now Asha had made the first move, but it was to reach out to him. He too was curious to know about her. He had hardly spoken to her during the one time they had met. Now, he kept his voice even and chatted with her casually as one did with an acquaintance.

Asha felt a sense of contentment after speaking to Asif. He seemed so sensible and mature for his age. He enquired about her without being intrusive. She sensed the unspoken question. When would she visit? She was not ready yet. He understood that without being told. He reassured her that he would always be there for her. Asha was glad she made the call.

And now she had to make another call. Till now, she had not conveyed anything about the birth issue to Ramesh. He had been busy preparing for and attending job interviews. He even had to travel out of town for some of the interviews. He got an all-expense paid trip for attending the second and third round of the interviews at the head office. He had just passed the third round of interviews for a plum job in a multinational company. The job was more or less in his pocket, he had assured her, and he was just waiting for appointment letter. He had already rejected a couple of job offers as the package was not up to his expectations or was getting posted to a remote place. But this was one job offer he was keenly looking forward to. He was entitled to family accommodation after the initial six month training period.

Asha decided it was time to convey to Ramesh about her birth issue. She met him as usual at the mall on Sunday. He had brought his dad's car and seemed to be in a good mood. He suggested a long drive, and she agreed. It would be nice to go somewhere quiet, where they would have some privacy.

As they cruised along the highway, Ramesh told her he had something to celebrate. He had just received the appointment letter for his dream job. There would be a six-month training period, and after that, he would be provided with fully furnished accommodation. He conveyed all this with enthusiasm to Asha. He was surprised to find her reaction so subdued. They were now strolling in the manicured lawns of a restaurant in the outskirts of the town. He had decided to splurge on an expensive restaurant to celebrate the job offer. He had asked Asha to choose, and she had selected the Chinese restaurant. It wasn't often that they left the confines of the mall. But today was special. He had to celebrate his first decent job offer. He wondered why Asha was not responding with her characteristic enthusiasm. Then he remembered. She had indicated during the phone call that she had something to convey to him. How insensitive of him! He had not given her a chance to talk. He had been so full of himself. She had a faraway look in her eyes. He squeezed her arm. 'You too had something to say,' he reminded her.

She was still silent. She did not know where to start. Ramesh seemed so happy. She hoped that this would not affect their relationship. Well, if it did, it was better now than later. Without realising, she had gravitated to the waterfall at the end of the lawn. It was here just a few months ago that she had gazed at the cascading waters with Nisha. And when she had turned, she had got the first glimpse of her biological family. She turned now, almost expecting to see them. Slowly, she walked towards the tables they had occupied earlier. Ramesh accompanied her quietly. He was giving her time to collect her thoughts. His initial surprise at her lack of enthusiasm had given way to apprehension. He wondered what was troubling her. She was having difficulty in expressing herself, and he gave her time.

As they seated themselves at the table, they were approached by a smiling waitress. She seemed to recognise

Asha and greeted her politely. After they had placed the order and the waitress had withdrawn, he remarked as such to Asha. That was the impetus she needed to open up.

'Yes, we came here a few months ago,' she said quietly. 'It was supposed to be a reunion with my dad's childhood friend.' She paused. 'But it turned out to be more than that.' Slowly, she related the entire story, right from the first phone call on her eighteenth birthday to the unexpected meeting with her birth parents at this very restaurant. Ramesh listened without interrupting. She paused when the waiter arrived with the food. They ate silently, each busy with their own thoughts.

Ramesh marvelled at her composure. At no time had she given him an inkling of the events unfolding in the past few months. She had at times looked anxious, but he had put it down to their surreptitious meetings. They had mutually decided to keep their affair under wraps till Nisha was hitched and he got a job. Now those two obstacles seemed to have been surmounted. Nisha was engaged, and her wedding was just a few months away. He had clinched a job with excellent prospects. He had been so busy in the search for a suitable job that he had neglected Asha. He had no idea so much had been going on in her life in the past few months. He felt a bit disappointed that she had not confided in him earlier. Reading his thoughts, Asha explained that she wanted time to face the issue. He nodded. Anyway, nothing could change his feelings for her. He loved her as a person, and it did not matter from whom or where she came. He reached out across the table and squeezed her hand.

'Don't worry, we will face the issue together,' he said.

Asha felt a burden lift from her shoulder. She smiled for the first time that evening. The waiter was happy to note that the young couple who ate their meal in a strained silence were now smiling as they ate the dessert. Must congratulate the pastry chef, he thought.

As Ramesh drove home after dropping Asha, he went over the conversation with her. He had wanted to convey the news of his job to her and then discuss about informing their respective parents. With a job in hand, he felt emboldened to talk to his parents and request them to approach the Khannas for their daughter's hand in marriage. Till now, his parents were clueless about his affair. Only his sister Neeta knew, and she had been sworn to secrecy. Now conveying the situation to his parents seemed a bit more complicated. One issue at a time, he decided. He had already told them about the job offer. His mom and dad were justifiably proud. Neeta glossed about the furnished accommodation that he would be provided. His mom declared that it was time he settled down.

'We will start searching for girls now,' she said gleefully.

This was the cue he needed. 'Well, actually I wanted to save you the trouble,' he said mischievously. 'I have already found one!' They were surprised. 'Who? When?' The questions came tumbling out.

Diffidently Ramesh explained. They were astonished. This had been going on under their nose, and they had not got a whiff of it till now. However, they were thrilled with his choice. They had known Asha since she was a little girl. They had a nodding acquaintance with her parents too.

Mrs Brinda Malhotra glanced at Neeta. She was smiling serenely.

'You knew about this?' she asked. Neeta nodded. 'And you never told us?'

'I discovered it by accident just a while ago.' Neeta justified herself.

They had managed to pull the wool over their eyes pretty neatly, thought Brinda.

'Anyway, congrats, Beta,' she said. Ramesh smiled happily, noting the approval in her voice.

'So what other secrets are you keeping from us?' she asked playfully.

'Well, that's it for now,' he replied smilingly. 'The darker secrets for later.'

She thought she detected a strange note in his voice when he said that, but she put it down to her imagination. This was such wonderful news, first the job and now a girl. Things seemed to be working for her son. Then why did she feel he had something more to say and was holding back?

Ramesh was deep in discussion with his dad. Ravinder was questioning him about the salary and perks of the job. He seemed satisfied with the package offered to his son. Brinda had to interrupt to get a word in. She suggested that they go together as a family to the Khanna residence to convey their marriage proposal.

Ramesh nodded his agreement. As expected, his parents had no objection to his betrothal to Asha. He wondered how that would change when they came to know about her birth issue. Well, he had to just hope for the best. He decided to break the news to them a little later. Let them first get used to Asha as a daughter-in-law, he thought. But of course, he should intimate his parents before they went to her house. He did not want them to learn about it there. One could never be certain of parents' reaction. He had to explain it to them calmly and gently.

He got an opportunity the following week. His mom had been talking about a niece of hers who was having difficulty conceiving and was planning to adopt a baby. After ten years of marriage, a few miscarriages and umpteen IVF procedures, the couple had finally given up on a genetic baby. They were now making the rounds of adoption centres, she related to her husband.

Ramesh had been idly listening as his mom was conveying all this to his dad. Hearing the words genetic baby, he got the cue to jump into the conversation.

'You know, Mom,' he said casually, 'Asha is not the genetic offspring of her parents.' There was a surprised silence. Both parents looked at him. They had hardly realised he was in the room, let alone following their conversation. It took some time for his statement to sink in.

'So she was adopted?' asked his mother.

'Not exactly,' he replied.

'Then what, a relative's child whom they adopted?' she asked confusedly. She recollected a cousin who had died while giving birth. The baby was brought up by a childless relative and had not been told she was adopted till even after her marriage. She had discovered it only after the death of her father, as she helped her mother sort out the papers.

'No, not really,' Ramesh shook his head.

'Well, then what?' asked Brinda, exasperated 'We have seen Asha since ages. She was with them since infancy.'

Ramesh hesitated. He did not know how much he should convey. He decided to make a plunge.

'She was accidentally exchanged at birth in the maternity home.'

Their faces expressed surprise. 'They discovered this inadvertently just about six months ago,' he added.

'And where are the birth parents?' enquired Brinda, when she found her voice.

'They are in Mumbai,' he said without elaborating. It took some time for them to digest the news. There was silence for a while.

Finally his mom asked, 'Since when have you known?'

'Asha told me a couple of weeks ago, Maa,' he said.

'Have you met the biolgical parents?' They wanted to know.

'No,' he replied truthfully. 'Asha too has met them only once. But their daughter has come to visit her birth parents and is staying with them right now.'

Neeta too had entered the room now and joined in the discussion. This information was news to her too. Asha had not confided in her about this latest happening in her life. For a best friend, she really kept a lot of secrets, thought Neeta.

'Bhaiya, that means Nisha is not her blood sister?' she asked.

'No, she is not,' he replied.

'So it must be the other girl I met during Nisha's engagement,' she said wonderingly. 'I did think Meena looked a lot like Nisha,' she added.

Brinda and Ravinder looked at each other. So Meena was the name of the exchanged baby, the genetic offspring of the Khannas. Well, the Khannas were probably dealing with it privately. It was not really their problem.

Ramesh explained to his parents that Asha had not yet informed her parents about him. She had been waiting for her elder sister, Nisha, to get fixed before speaking about him.

'Now that Nisha is engaged, the line is clear,' teased Neeta.

'Anyway, Beta,' said Ranvir, 'If her parents agree, I have no objection to the match.'

Brinda nodded. 'But her birth parents too should be informed,' she said.

CHAPTER 21

$\mathcal{A}$sha was now tasked with the difficult job of informing her parents about Ramesh. He had fulfilled his end of the bargain by conveying about her to his parents as soon as he landed a job. They had approved and were eager to visit her household to formally ask for her hand in marriage.

She had promised Ramesh that she would inform her parents as soon as Nisha's engagement was done. But now, she was seized with panic. There were so many other issues involved. She still had to come to terms that they were not her birth parents.

Tentatively she decided to break the news to her mother first. As she helped her mom to clear the dinner table, she picked up the courage.

'Neeta's parents want to visit us next week,' she stated offhand.

Something in her voice warned Seema that it was not to be an ordinary visit. She looked askance at Asha. Slowly Asha confided in her mom. She told her about the initial meetings with Ramesh and how the casual friendship grew to a serious relationship. Her mom was surprised. Asha's long absences at the mall now seemed clear.

'Why didn't you tell me before?' she asked gently.

'I wanted Nisha to be settled first before I spoke about it,' Asha replied softly. 'Also, Ramesh wanted to get a job before he informed his parents. Now that he has landed a job, he wants to come here with his parents.'

'I will discuss it with your dad,' said Seema. 'You are still very young. Nisha, who is four years older than you, has just got engaged.'

Anil was astonished as Seema revealed her conversation with Asha. The impending visit of Ramesh with his parents showed they were serious. He had no objection to the match. Ramesh was a fine young man. But both were far too young to make such decisions, he mused.

Then Anil grew thoughtful. He would have to inform Fareed and Salma. They had a right to know. He had a heart-to-heart talk with Asha. He then broached the topic of informing her biological parents.

Asha was so happy about getting the matter off her chest and her parents' approval that she was ready to agree to anything. She was even willing to visit the Khan household in Mumbai. They had pleaded with Anil that they would like to get to know her before she was married off. It was a reasonable request. Asha too was curious to know about them. And she wanted to establish a rapport with Asif. It was decided that she would visit the following weekend. Anil would drop her on Friday evening. And Asif would drive her back on Sunday. He would then take back Ameena whose holidays were coming to a close.

Nisha was thrilled to know about Ramesh and Asha but miffed that she had not guessed earlier. She recollected how he had been so diffident to enter the house on Asha's eighteenth birthday. She had to really urge him to come in and have the cake. Such duplicity!

Anyway, he seemed a nice guy. She was happy for her sister. And then she thought about her new sister. She had to help her sort out the tangle. First, she had to requisition the help of her mom and dad. They would have to gently convey it to Meena's parents. Asif was scheduled to visit them next week to drop Asha and pick up Meena. Maybe, he could be sounded on the situation when he was here. He could help convey it to his parents as diplomatically as posible.

Neeta resolved to discuss the issue with her mother. She cornered her after dinner. Seema was still full of Asha and Ramesh. Slowly, Nisha veered the conversation to Meena. She too has found her life partner but has not told her parents, she informed her mom.

'She is also too young,' said Seema emphatically.

'That is not the problem,' said Nisha, carefully choosing her words.

'Then what, the boy is not settled yet?' asked her mom.

'Well, he will be next year,' replied Nisha. 'But that is not the problem.'

'Then what is it?' asked her mom, intrigued.

'He is not a Muslim,' said Nisha quietly.

Slowly Nisha recounted the trekking trips that Ameena had gone with her brother Asif and his friends and how she had gotten close to Rohit. Her mom grew thoughtful.

This was something she had not thought of. She further enquired about Rohit and his family background. Nisha informed her that he was in the final year of a master's degree in engineering. He had already been selected during campus interviews for placement in a top multinational company. Both his parents were doctors. His father headed the Ophthalmology Department in a medical college. His mother was a general practitioner. They hailed from Hyderabad. Shoib and he were friends since their schooldays at Hyderabad. There was a prevalence of what locals called *Ganga Jamuna* culture in Hyderabad. The mix of Hindu-Muslim culture was referred to as *Ganga-jamunai* in Hyderabad. It meant that like the confluence of the two rivers, the two communities blended smoothly in the city. Shoib was the only one who knew about the situation, and he dutifully covered for Ameena and his best friend Rohit.

Ameena's family, explained Nisha, thought she was friendly to Shoib and would have no objections on that score. But Rohit was a different matter. Seema understood the delicate situation. It would have to be handled with sensitivity.

CHAPTER 22

The following weekend, Anil and Seema drove to Mumbai. They met Salma and Fareed at their tastefully decorated flat. They did not stay for a meal citing a prior commitment. Since Asha was staying for just a couple of days, they did not want to impinge on their time with her.

Asha was elated that her affair with Ramesh was now in the open and met with both parents' approval. She felt she could face anything now. And she really wanted to spend some time with Asif.

They had a quiet dinner after her arrival. Salma noted her gentle mannerisms. She was so like Asif, with long eyelashes and delicate countenance. The dinner conversation was muted. Fareed and Salma did not pry her with questions. After dinner, she spent time chatting with Asif. She told him about her college, friends, the books she had read, and the latest movies she had seen. Asif and she seemed to hit it off, noted Fareed. There was no bantering like with Ameena. They both seemed to be on the same wavelength, liking the same things.

The next day, his sister Tasneem came to visit. She wanted to meet the new addition to the family. She hugged Asha and examined her face minutely, looking for family resemblances. She insisted on calling her Aisha. Post-lunch, she had a long discussion with Fareed and Salma. Asif and Asha had gone out for a movie at a multiplex.

Tasneem requested Fareed that he take steps to initiate Asha into the Muslim faith. She suggested that he make arrangements for her to take Koran classes and that he change her name to Aisha. She offered to bring Maulvi Barkatullah, imam of the Big Mosque, the Bari Masjid, to perform the conversion. Fareed was aghast at her suggestions.

'*Aapa*, what if they insist that Ameena turn into a Hindu?' he countered.

'Ameena is already following the tenets of Islam. She will not deviate from the true path,' replied Tasneem.

'*La ilaha il-allah, Muhammad ur-Rasool Allah.* There is no God but Allah, and Muhammad is his apostle. It is our duty to enlighten Aisha also. I am sure she will be receptive,' added Tasneem.

Fareed looked doubtful.

'When so many non-Muslims have converted,' explained Tasneem, 'what is the objection for someone who has been born in the Muslim faith to reaffirm the beliefs?' She reiterated that the conversion of one non-believer to Islam was enough to ensure a place in the first of eight heavens—*Jannat Ul Khuld* (garden of eternity).

Fareed nodded his head but still looked uncomfortable.

'You will be failing in your duty if you do not make the effort,' warned Tasneem before departing.

When Asha and Fareed returned, it was too late to have a discussion. Next morning, Salma and Fareed had a quiet talk with Asha. They told her that since she was born into a Muslim family, it behoved them to explain the tenets of the Muslim faith to her. After that, it was her decision to accept the religion of her birth. Fareed gently explained that it was illegal to forcibly convert anyone to the true faith. You are welcome into the redeeming radiance of Allah only if you come by free will. It is clearly said in the Holy Koran, *La ikraha fi ad-deen.* Let there be no compulsion in religion. If you do not see the light, then the Koran lets you go your way. *Lakun dinakum wa-la-yeddin*—Your religion is for you and mine is for me.

Asha grew thoughtful. She did not want to hurt them. They had conveyed the request gently. They said that they would respect her decision. All they wanted was a patient hearing. In a way, this was what she had been dreading, being asked to choose. Years of conditioning had left her wary of the other faith. She had visited her biological parents to get to know them once before her marriage and of course to establish a rapport with Asif. After her marriage, she would in any case be a guest in either parental house. Her future was with Ramesh. She could not afford to make a unilateral decision. The fact was that she had never paid much attention to religion. While her household celebrated all the festivals with gusto, visits to the temple or chanting of the bhajans was a rarity. Except for the customary visit before a board exam, she had never gone on her own volition to the temple. Her mom too was not overzealous like some of their family friends and neighbours. She had never conducted bhajans or kirtans in the house but always attended the sessions when neighbours invited her. She lit the *diya* daily in the house and said the evening prayers for the entire family. As kids, Asha and Nisha used to join her for the daily evening prayer. As they grew older, they were busy with tuitions or class project during the evening prayer time and more often than not missed it. Their mom did not insist, and now, it was a rarity for them to join her for the evening prayer. It was only on festive occasions that they made the effort.

Thus, Asha had no intention of following the rituals of any religion, neither the one she had been raised in nor the one she was born into. She confided in Asif that she was loath to change her beliefs. Asif was perturbed to learn that she had even been asked to do so by his parents. He confronted them the next day. He questioned his dad on the wisdom of persuading her to change her religion. Fareed replied that he was only doing his duty.

'No point in creating more problems in her life,' said Asif. His parents nodded mutely.

'It was a bad idea from the beginning,' agreed Fareed. 'If it was not for Tasneem's urgings, we would never have raised the topic.'

Asif mused over the dilemma that Asha was placed in. He assured her that she would not face such requests in future from his parents. He was driving back to Pune with her. He had to pick up Ameena on his way back. She assured him that she was not offended by the request of his parents.

'It's just that I am in any case not a religious person. I don't see the point in moving from one to another.'

'I agree with you. Don't give it another thought,' said Asif comfortingly as they drove into the Khanna driveway. The entire family was waiting for them. Asif greeted them all courteously. He did not stay long citing the long journey ahead. He helped Ameena load her suitcase into the car, and they departed soon after but not before a round of hugs and handshakes.

'So you had a good time,' he enquired good-naturedly.

'Mmmm! So how was Asha's stay with you guys?'

'All fine. Tasneem bua visited us. She insisted on calling her Aisha.'

'Even they called me Meena,' giggled Ameena.

'Not only that. Tasneem bua urged Abba to talk to Asha about accepting the Muslim faith.'

'And did Abba do so?' asked Ameena, all ears now.

'Well, he reluctantly did convey the request. Asha listened quietly. But then on reflection, she decided she was not interested in jumping ship. She is going to marry a Ramesh. It would complicate matters with the boy's family if she stresses over her birth religion.' Ameena listened thoughtfully.

In her case, it would help smoothen matters with the boy's family, she thought. But first, she had to convey the situation to her own family. She dreaded the scene. She decided to confide in Asif first. She had the sudden urge to do so there and then. But then, he was driving. She did not know what his reaction would be. He could get agitated. He might fumble at the wheel. It had been a long day.

Prudence is the better part of valour. It was better to hold her tongue until a more opportune time. They arrived pretty late at Mumbai. Her parents were waiting anxiously. They were full of questions regarding her stay. She told them everything except what was uppermost in her mind.

If they had wished Asha to accept the religion of her birth, would they be receptive to her marrying into the faith of her birth? The question trembled on Ameena's lips, but she could not bring herself to mouth the words. She answered their queries and bid them good night.

Ameena had a disturbed sleep. The matter was weighing heavily on her mind, and it brought an uncharacteristic frown to her face. Her mother noticed it during breakfast time but did not comment. She, however, questioned Asif if all had gone well during her stay at the Khanna household. Asif assured her that she had enjoyed her stay there and faced no problem whatsoever. In fact, she was raring to go again, he informed his mom. In the evening, Asif casually related his mom's apprehension to Ameena.

'She thinks that you are perturbed because you are confused about your identity,' said Asif.

Ameena listened quietly. It was time to speak up, she decided. Slowly, hesitantly, she told Asif about how her friendship with Rohit had deepened into a desire to spend her life with him.

Asif was flabbergasted. All this had been happening under his nose and he had been totally unaware. His face darkened. Rohit had something to answer for. Shoib too, he thought grimly. Shoib must have known and had covered up for Rohit all this time. They had been pals since childhood.

Ameena could see the rage on Asif's face. It was the first time she had seen him so angry. It probably had something to do with him being out of the loop and unaware of what had been brewing under his nose. He probably blamed himself for succumbing to her pleas to join his trek group.

Ameena sat quietly, eyes downcast. The fight had gone out of her. She was too weary to give explanations. She knew it was a shock for Asif, as it would be for her parents. But it had to come out some time. Better now than later. She had to steel herself for the verbal onslaughts, for the arguments, explanations, and discussions. She sighed.

Noting Ameena's uncharacteristic sober demeanour, Asif's anger dissipated. She had gone through a lot in the past few months, he realised, from getting to know she had been exchanged at birth to this secret that had been weighing on her. He could not be harsh with her at this trying time of her life. God knew she had faced many more hurdles.

He got up and put his arm round her shoulders. 'Don't worry, Sis, we will handle the situation.' She looked up, surprised. Her eyes filled with tears as she realised Asif was no longer angry. A wave of relief swept over her. She had an ally as she would convey the news to her parents.

Eventually, she did not have to face the ordeal of conveying it. Asif told them gently the next day. They were surprised and shocked. But they had gone through so much in the past few months that their reaction was subdued. They ruminated over how they had been busy trying to convince Asha to accept their faith, the one she had been born into.

The daughter they had raised had already chosen her path, even before knowing her antecedents. It was her blood calling, sagely observed Tasneem as they told her the next day. They pondered over how to handle the situation. They could not precipitate a crisis by barring her from seeing Rohit. She was now legally an adult. That would have counted for nothing if she was their biological daughter. But now things were a bit different. The circumstances of her birth had changed the equation. They could not intimidate her in the choice of her life partner. They had to accept the inevitable.

Ameena was pleasantly surprised to find that her parents did not voice their objections to Rohit. If truth be told, Rohit was fine in all respects, except for the difference in the religion. He was well-educated and came from a respectable family background. He was polite, courteous to elders and a soft spoken young man.

Ameena called Rohit the next morning. She informed him that Asif and her parents were aware of his presence in her life.

'Did they give you a hard time,' he enquired.

'Not as much as I expected,' she replied.

The peculiar circumstances of her birth must have helped mitigate their objection, thought Rohit.

It was time to inform his parents too. He knew objections would be raised as soon as they heard her name. He got a brainwave: Why not inform them about her using the new name, the one her biological parents called her? It would have to be done delicately, at an opportune time.

A couple of days later, his mom, Radha, again raised the topic of his marriage. Her relatives had been mentioning about some good matches. She was armed with a couple of photos with biodata on the reverse side.

'Ma, I told you I have already found a girl,' said Rohit, irritated.

'Is it so? You have never told us much about her. When are you going to introduce us?'

'Soon, Ma,' he replied. 'She too has to inform her parents about us.'

'You are a good catch for any family,' she replied smugly. 'I am sure her parents won't have any objections for you.'

'Oh there will always be issues,' he warned.

'Where are they from and what is her name?' asked his mom.

'They live in Mumbai. She is called Meena,' he replied cautiously.

'Nice name,' said his mom.

Rohit winced.

CHAPTER 23

*A*sha was happy to be back in her home. Her parents queried her about her stay in Mumbai. She gave all the details but left out the request made by her biological parents for her to accept their faith.

However, as she was chatting with Ramesh the next day, she confided in him.

'My biological parents want me to accept their faith,' she told him tentatively.

'What do you want to do?' he asked concerned.

'I have read extensively about all the religions. I am really curious about the rituals followed in different religions, but only in the academic sense. I am not interested in following the rituals of any religion.'

Ramesh relaxed visibly.

'Would it be a problem?' she asked him.

'No,' he said emphatically. 'Not from my side.'

She looked enquiringly at him.

'But my mom could have issues.'

That was true. As soon as Brinda was made aware of the issue, she was wary. She expressed her apprehension to Ravinder.

'I did not expect a Muslim daughter-in-law,' she said indignantly to her husband. 'What would our relatives say? This would affect Neeta too. She will not get any marriage proposals from our community.'

'Nothing like that,' he assured her. 'Asha has been raised in a Hindu household. As Ramesh says, she has shown no inclination to change her faith.'

Brinda did not look convinced. 'Her biological parents could put pressure and convince her.'

'She has already refused to look into a change of religion.' explained Ravinder

'And who would do the *kanyadaan*?' she asked Ramesh.

'Mom, it will be done by the Khannas. You won't have to give any explanations to your friends.'

'It's not that, Beta. We have to think about Neeta's marriage too. If people know you have married a Muslim girl, it will be a scandal, and your sister will not get any proposals.'

'Mom,' remonstrated Ramesh, 'this should not affect Neeta at all.'

'You can get the best of proposals from our community.'

'I want to be with her only. I don't care about the religion she was born or raised in.'

Brinda looked miffed. 'And what if at a later date if she changes her mind and decides to adopt the religion of her real parents?' she asked.

Ramesh shrugged. 'We don't know what would happen at a later date,' he informed her. 'Tomorrow if you realised I had been exchanged as a baby, would you abandon me?'

Brinda smiled. 'You couldn't be an exchanged baby. You are stubborn as your dad.'

'Mom,' said Neeta mischievously, 'if Priya Aunty just realised that she were born in a Muslim household, I wonder how she would react.'

Her mom looked at her blankly. Ramesh smiled. Their neighbour, Priya, was a devout and pious middle-aged lady. She always wore a massive bindi on her forehead. She organised bhajans in her household every weekend. She religiously performed all the *Pujas* for the various Gods and Goddesses that adorned her prayer room. She offered the Brahmin's prayer daily to the Sun God, the *Gayatri Mantra*. The twenty-four syllables of this mantra were the holiest of the verses of the Rig Veda. They had emerged from the mouth of Brahma.

> *Om bhurbhuva swaha!*
> *Tat Savitoor varenyam*
> *Bhargodevasya dhimahi*
> *Dhiyo yo nah prachodayat!*

We meditate on the unique light of the divine Sun, with which we illuminate our minds!

She repeated this twenty-four times a day at dawn. Each sunset, in the silence of her home, she recited her prayers until the first stars became a sprinkle on the western sky.

She was as devout as they came. This got Ramesh thinking into the motivation of religious beliefs. Does one believe in a religion only because they are born into it? If one was raised in a particular religion, does the discovery of being the product of another religion change your line of thinking?

Would the devout, bhajan-chanting fifty-year-old neighbour lady go silent on learning she was born into another faith? Would she wipe the vermilion off her forehead if blood tests proved she was born into another religion? Would she banish all the idols from her house? And more importantly, would the chanting of devotional songs still bring peace to her soul? Or would she now be immune to the soporific effects of the daily chants? Would she consider it a sacrilege to keep idols at home?

And would the veiled lady, saying her prayers five times a day, shrug off her scarf? Would she now decorate her house with idols and fold her hands reverently in prayers? And the lady with a large dot on her forehead could wipe it off with a flick of her wrist, but would it be possible to shake the beliefs of a lifetime with a flick of her head?

Are one's beliefs a product of one's upbringing? Realising you belong to another set of parents is not as cataclysmic as suddenly realising you belong to another religion. A person does not choose his religion at birth nor do they have a chance to choose as they near adulthood. They could choose their life partner or career. They could even change their country or citizenship with impunity. One could easily adapt to the rules and regulations of a new county. But changing a religion is another ball game. A person could lackadaisically accept the birth religion. But one has to be really committed or convinced to change into different religion.

Brinda realised that Ramesh was serious about continuing his relationship with Asha.

Neither Ravinder nor her daughter felt anything amiss in the relationship. She decided to give in.

Ramesh was happy he had the approval of his mom finally. Maybe the scenario that Neeta described had helped change her mind. Whatever the reason, it was time for celebration. He rang up Asha and told her he had the approval of his mom and dad, even after they knew of all the facts. Asha was elated. It was nice to know her future mother-in-law did not have any reservations on that score. She conveyed the same to her mom and sis. Both were happy for her, but Nisha grew thoughtful. It was time to convince Ameena's in-laws also. Ameena had conveyed to her that now her parents knew of her situation. They had not given her a hard time, probably taking into consideration all that she had gone through in the past few months. Now the only hurdle that remained was for Rohit to convey to his parents and get their approval.

CHAPTER 24

Seema and Anil expressed their desire to meet Rohit. At Nisha's insistence, Ameena agreed to bring him to Pune during the weekend. Instead of a trekking trip, the foursome decided to drive down to Pune. Shoib had been in on the whole thing since the beginning. He nudged Rohit.

'You will have two sets of in-laws,' he grinned.

'The more the merrier,' shot back Rohit.

They arrived just in time for lunch. Seema beamed with happiness on meeting Rohit. He seemed a fine and decent young man. She had been busy whole morning preparing dishes in the kitchen. She singled Rohit out for her attention and served him extra-large helpings. Shoib smirked.

'I can see you doubling in size soon with this double in-law thing,' he whispered.

'The other set of in-laws would probably like to cut me up and serve my guts.'

'Yep, your head on a platter would make their day.'

Their whispered conversation was cut short with the arrival of Anil. He had taken a break from office to join them for lunch. He conversed amicably with the youngsters. They discussed their future job prospects and the growing unemployment in the country.

After lunch, Anil took Rohit to his study. He had a frank talk with him. Rohit assured him that he was committed to Ameena. He admitted that he still had to convince his parents. He would do that as soon as possible. Anil offered to talk to them if needed, but Rohit said he would handle it.

The group departed after the evening tea. The drive back was pleasant. All were in high spirits. Their conversation was littered with merriment. Ameena recollected the drive back just a few weeks ago.

She had been feeling miserable and guilty. She had been then searching for words to convey to Asif about her relationship with Rohit. She had been dreading his reaction.

Eventually, he had accepted the situation and even convinced his parents so that they would not give her a hard time. She would be eternally grateful to him for that. Today, she felt all was right with the world. She was surrounded with love. She felt the circle of her life complete. The only hurdle now was for Rohit's parents to accept her. He had promised to speak to them soon.

Rohit found it more difficult than expected to handle his parents. He seemed to have started out on the wrong foot. It was during breakfast, a couple of days later, that his mom again raised the topic of his marriage. She queried about the mystery girl he was in love with and asked when she would get an opportunity to meet her. She wondered aloud whether she really existed or he had made up the story to ward off unwanted proposals. Rohit replied without making an effort to cushion the shock.

'You have met her. She is Asif's sister.'

There was a shocked silence. His dad put down the newspaper. He wondered if he had heard right. When his mom finally found her voice, she asked him if he was joking. He shook his head.

'You said her name was Meena,' she said accusingly.

'It sort of is,' he said sheepishly. Radha looked confused. Slowly, Rohit explained that Ameena was the biological daughter of the Khannas. He described how she had been exchanged at birth at the maternity nursing home.

'The matter has been discovered just recently. She has established contact with her biological parents. She is called Meena in their household,' he added by way of explanation.

His mom was still not happy. 'She has been raised in a different faith. She will always have their teachings embedded in her.'

'It does not matter,' said Rohit with finality. 'I had loved her even before I knew about the birth issue.'

'You mean you would have gone ahead even then?' Radha wailed. She looked towards her husband for support. Professor Mohan Rao cleared his throat.

'Son, do you think you are making the right decision,' he asked calmly.

'Papa, I am sure. Her religion does not matter to me.'

'But it does to us,' his father retorted. 'How do we explain to our relatives that our eldest son, our firstborn, has broken tradition and married outside?'

'It happens, Papa. You could accept my friendship with Shoib. Why can't you accept my relationship with Ameena.'

'It is not the same thing,' his dad explained patiently. 'Ameena and you will have kids. She will instruct them in her teachings. They will be confused a lot.'

'No, Papa. They will be exposed to both the teachings. They can have the best of both worlds.'

His mother interjected now, 'You said she was called Meena in her birth parents' house. Would she be reverting to the religion she was born into?'

'No,' said Rohit. 'Neither her biological parents have asked her to do so, nor would I.'

Ameena and he had discussed it. While she loved the new name, she had no interest in abandoning her faith. It was not just that the parents who raised her would be hurt. She could not forget a lifetime of religious teachings. They were embedded in her psyche. It was not that she was overtly religious. In fact, she had rebelled against some of the strictures of her religion, especially when she felt it was unfair to her sex.

But then her father had been broad-minded. He had given her the freedom to do as she liked in most things. He had never differentiated between his son and daughter. He treated them both equally. Asif and she had both studied in convent schools known for their emphasis on excellent education. Simultaneously, a *maulvi* had come home to take Koran classes. She was well versed in the Koran and had also read the Bible during her schooldays. The school day had started with the Christian prayer.

*'Our Father who art in heaven, Hallowed be
    Thy Name,
Thy Kingdom come, Thy will be done,
On Earth as it is in Heaven
Give us today our Daily Bread, and forgive
    us our Sins,
As we forgive each one of those who sins
    against us'*

Even now, the familiar refrain rang in her ears. She could juxtapose herself with ease into both the faiths. There would be no dichotomy in maintaining her faith in Rohit's household, she felt.

Rohit agreed with her that it was a non-issue. But his parents did not see it as such. They had seemed so open and broad-minded. They had close friends from different religions. Shoib and he had literally grown up in each other's house. But they balked at having a daughter-in-law from that faith.

Rohit sighed. It would take a lot more to convince his parents. It looked like he would have to enlist the help of Mr Khanna. It happened that Mr Khanna was visiting Mumbai the following week on a business trip. He expressed a desire to meet Rohit's parents.

Professor Rao greeted him courteously. As the nature of his business became apparent, he became wary. However, Mr Khanna turned on the charm offensive.

'I have not done anything for this daughter of mine,' he explained. 'I inadvertently lost her soon after her birth. She was raised and nurtured by another family. Just when she has re-entered my life, it is time for her to step into a new life.' Mohan Rao remained silent.

'She is on the threshold of her new life,' continued Anil. 'And I would do anything to help smoothen her path.'

'I understand and sympathise with your situation,' replied Prof Rao, 'but I envisage problems. My aged parents will be shocked. My younger son and daughter will be affected. Even distant relatives will snigger.'

Anil listened with equanimity. 'I know how relatives react. I agree it will not be easy to quell the wagging tongues. I have spoken to Mr Fareed. He has agreed that I can perform the marriage and give away Meena during the wedding ceremony.'

Mohan Rao looked thoughtful. He glanced at Rohit's anxious face. He made a decision. 'I think I can convince my wife,' he said finally.

Rohit was elated. Mr Khanna had accomplished what he had considered an insurmountable problem. Mr Khanna had convinced his dad with his generous offer to perform the wedding ceremonies and give away the bride. The Khanna's would do the *Kanyadaan*. His dad had run out of objections to the match and gave in gracefully. His mom would be a cakewalk now. As expected, she deferred to the wishes of her husband and son. She was outnumbered.

Rohit immediately contacted Ameena and gave her the good news. As the details of the conversation between Mr Khanna and Prof Mohan Rao were conveyed, her eyes filled with tears. Her birth parents had offered to bear all the expenses of the wedding. They wished to give her a grand wedding to make up for their absence in her life. And the fact that she would be married off from the Khanna household had convinced Rohit's parents to give their acceptance. They agreed that her faith was her personal affair and that they would not have a say on that issue. Ameena was grateful to them on that score.

But she reserved her greatest admiration and respect for her parents, the ones who had raised her. Her affection for them surged. They had nurtured her from infancy to adulthood. They had given her so much love and affection, which she had taken for granted all along. And when the time came to let her go, they did so without a murmur. Whether she wanted to be with her biological parents or marry the person of her choice. They had accepted with equanimity that the life partner she chose did not belong to their faith. They had not said a word on that score. Suddenly, the inane words she frequently saw on coffee cups at the swanky gift stores, 'World's Best Parents' made sense.

CHAPTER 25

S alma and Fareed were surprised to receive a gift of a silver plate during breakfast. At the bottom was engraved, 'World's Best Parents'. Was there any other kind of parent? thought Fareed.

Anil and Seema were discussing the marriage arrangements for Nisha. Rekha was in the thick of things. She was busy planning and giving instructions. She revelled in the role of a wedding planner.

'Don't expend all your energy on this one,' warned Seema. 'You have two more weddings to plan this year.' It had been decided that after Nisha's wedding, they would perform Ameena's wedding a couple of months later. And soon after that, it would be Asha and Ramesh's wedding.

'I guess I can get heavy discounts during Rohit and Meena's wedding,' joked Rekha. 'By the time Asha and Ramesh get married, I will be a pro. I can start a business as a wedding planner!'